THE UMI ANNUAL COMMENTARY 2022–2023

PRECEPTS FOR LIVING®

PERSONAL STUDY GUIDE

MISSION STATEMENT

We are called
of God to create, produce, and distribute
quality Christian education products;
to deliver exemplary customer service;
and to provide quality Christian
educational services, which will empower
God's people, especially within the Black
community, to evangelize, disciple,
and equip people for serving Christ,
His kingdom, and church.

Precepts For Living® Personal Study Guide, Vol. 22, September 2022–August 2023. Published annually by UMI (Urban Ministries, Inc.), P.O. Box 436987, Chicago, IL 60643-6987. Founder: Melvin E. Banks Sr., LittD; CEO: C. Jeffrey Wright, JD; Managing Editor: Daschell M. Hills, MS; Developmental Editor: Adriana Rivera, MDiv; Editors/Writers: Evangeline Carey and DeVona Alleyne. $9.95 per copy. Printed in the U.S.A. **To order:** Contact your local Christian bookstore; call UMI at **1-800-860-8642**; or visit our web site at www.urbanministries.com.

SEPTEMBER 2022–AUGUST 2023

TABLE OF CONTENTS

PRECEPTS FOR LIVING® PERSONAL STUDY GUIDE

SEPTEMBER 2022–AUGUST 2023

TABLE OF CONTENTS

PRECEPTS FOR LIVING® PERSONAL STUDY GUIDE

INTRODUCTION

Welcome to the *Precepts For Living®* Personal Study Guide! While using it, we hope that you will find it to be an enlightening and rewarding experience. This study guide can be used as a reference tool for any teacher or student who is serious about learning and knowing the inspired Word of God. It is designed to be used in conjunction with the *Precepts For Living®* Annual Commentary. It should help you get the God-intended meaning of each Scripture presented and explained in the commentary. Therefore, it is suggested that you use the guide in the following way:

- Thoroughly study each lesson in the *Precepts For Living®* Annual Commentary. Go to the companion lesson in this study guide and answer all the questions pertaining to the lesson.
- After you have answered all the questions for a particular lesson on your own, check your answers by using the answer key, which is found in the back of this book.
- If you miss an answer, go back and research it in the *Precepts For Living®* Annual Commentary. This will enhance both your learning experience and memorization of Scripture.

Enjoy this *Precepts For Living®* Personal Study Guide. As you do your Bible study, observe Scripture, grasp it by correctly interpreting the text, and then walk in the knowledge of God's Word.

"Let us hold fast the profession of our faith without wavering (for he is faithful that promised)" (Hebrews 10:23).

SEPTEMBER 4, 2022

FAITH CALLS FOR PERSEVERANCE

HEBREWS 10:19–31

Use with Bible Study Guide 1.

WORDS, PHRASES, AND DEFINITIONS

Write the definition of the following words.

1. adversaries: ____________________
2. apostasy: ____________________
3. "a true heart": ____________________
4. common: ____________________
5. "God's adversaries": ____________________
6. "hold fast": ____________________
7. insult: ____________________
8. provoke: ____________________
9. "the blood of the covenant": ____________________
10. "The day": ____________________

JUMP-STARTING THE LESSON

11. In the In Focus story, why did Angie feel that Anthony could not really love her?

____

____

____

____

12. Through ____________________ in ____________________, our sins are ____________________ and we have a ____________________ (see In Focus).

UNDERSTANDING THE LESSON

13. Where was the ***Holy of Holies*** located in the Temple (see The People, Places, and Times)? ______________

____

14. The author of the book of Hebrews argued the superiority of ____________________ and ____________________ (see The People, Places, and Times).

15. What happened on the ***Day of Atonement*** (see Background)? ______________________________

____

____

16. Through the shed blood of Christ, we can come before our Creator by ______________________ (Hebrews 10:19–21, In Depth, More Light on the Text).

17. List two ways in which we should approach the throne of grace (of God) (Hebrews 10:19–21, More Light on the Text).

    a. ____

    b. ____

18. List three indictments of an ***apostate*** (Hebrews 10:28–29, More Light on the Text).

    a. ____

    b. ____

    c. ____

COMMITTING TO THE WORD

19. Memorize and write Hebrews 10:19–24 (KJV) verbatim.

____

____

____

WALKING IN THE WORD

20. On the lines below, express your appreciation for ***the great and wonderful salvation*** that Jesus Christ brought to believers.

____

____

____

"Now faith is the substance of things hoped for, the evidence of things not seen" (Hebrews 11:1).

SEPTEMBER 11, 2022

FAITH IS ASSURANCE

HEBREWS 11:1–3, 6; PSALM 46:1–3, 8–11

Use with Bible Study Guide 2.

WORDS, PHRASES, AND DEFINITIONS

Match the words, phrases, or names with the correct definitions.

1. _____ Asaph
2. _____ elders
3. _____ Enoch
4. _____ evidence
5. _____ faith
6. _____ refuge
7. _____ sons of Korah
8. _____ substance
9. _____ *tehillim*
10. _____ *tephillot*

a. belief with the predominant ideas of trust or confidence; assurance

b. temple musicians and assistants in the Jewish culture

c. the Hebrew word that most of the psalms are, which means "prayers"

d. a shelter from rain, storm, or danger; where one finds rest and asylum

e. the traditional Hebrew title for the Psalms that means "praises"

f. individuals with attested age or dignity

g. one of the writers of the Psalms

h. proof or test

i. It means that faith makes the things believers hope for real.

j. one who pleased God because of his faith

JUMP-STARTING THE LESSON

11. Why was Professor Williams so excited by Deshawn's answer to the question she asked the class (see In Focus)? ____

____

____

____

12. According to the In Focus story, ____________________ is necessary to ____________________ and ____________________ on God's strength.

UNDERSTANDING THE LESSON

13. List seven writers of the book of Psalms (see The People, Places, and Times).

a. ______________________ b. ______________________

c. ______________________ d. ______________________

e. ______________________ f. ______________________

g. ______________________

14. The book of Psalms was written over a period of how many years (see The People, Places, and Times)?

a. 10 b. 25 c. 50 d. 100 e. 200 f. 1,000

15. List three reasons why the Jewish Christians considered giving up Christianity and returning to Judaism (see Background).

a. ______________________

b. ______________________

c. ______________________

16. What does faith reveal (Hebrews 11:6, In Depth)? ______________________

17. Faith is trust in God as our ______________________ (Psalm 46:1–3, In Depth).

18. Without faith, it is ______________________ to please God (Hebrews 11:6, In Depth, More Light on the Text).

COMMITTING TO THE WORD

19. Memorize and write verbatim Hebrews 11:1 and Psalm 46:1–3.

Hebrews 11:1 ______________________

Psalm 46:1–3 ______________________

WALKING IN THE WORD

20. Share a time or incident where you ***walked by faith***.

> *"Wherefore seeing we also are compassed about with so great a cloud of witnesses, let us lay aside every weight, and the sin which doth so easily beset us, and let us run with patience the race that is set before us, Looking unto Jesus the author and finisher of our faith; who for the joy that was set before him endured the cross, despising the shame, and is set down at the right hand of the throne of God" (Hebrews 12:1–2).*

SEPTEMBER 18, 2022

FAITH IS ENDURANCE

HEBREWS 12:1–11

Use with Bible Study Guide 3.

WORDS, PHRASES, AND DEFINITIONS

Define or identify.

1. Alexandria: ______________________________
2. chastening: ______________________________
3. faith: ______________________________
4. "Jesus is the 'finisher' of our faith": ______________________________
5. patience: ______________________________
6. perseverance: ______________________________
7. Rome: ______________________________
8. sin: ______________________________
9. profit: ______________________________
10. witness: ______________________________

JUMP-STARTING THE LESSON

11. Before taking the action steps needed to prepare for the 5K race, what did Regina do (see In Focus)? ______

____

____

UNDERSTANDING THE LESSON

12. List two reasons why the author of Hebrews wrote his letter (see Background).

 a. ______________________________

 b. ______________________________

13. The writer of Hebrews suggests that all Christians emulate Jesus' ____________________ and ____________________ if they anticipate an eternal reward (see Background).

14. Who is the ***ultimate model*** of perseverance (Hebrews 12:1–2, In Depth)? ____________________

15. How do we ***acquire endurance*** (Hebrews 12:3–6, In Depth, More Light on the Text)? ____________________

____

16. According to Hebrews 12:5, how should we view ***trials suffered for righteousness' sake*** (In Depth, More Light on the Text)? ____________________

____

17. What is God's ***long-range goal*** in disciplining believers (Hebrews 12:10, More Light on the Text)?

____

____

18. According to Hebrews 12:11, what is the purpose of the believer's pain (More Light on the Text)?

____

____

COMMITTING TO THE WORD

19. Fill in the blanks.

"Wherefore seeing we also are ____________________ about with so ____________________ a cloud of ____________________, let us ____________________ ____________________ every ____________________, and the ____________________ which doth so easily beset us, and let us ____________________ with ____________________ the ____________________ that is set before us, Looking unto ____________________ the ____________________ and ____________________ of our faith; who for the ____________________ that was set before him endured the ____________________, despising the ____________________, and is set down at the ____________________ ____________________ of the throne of ____________________" (Hebrews 12:1–2).

WALKING IN THE WORD

20. Share what Hebrews 12:1–2 means to you and ***your walk with the Lord***.

____

____

____

"Wherefore we receiving a kingdom which cannot be moved, let us have grace, whereby we may serve God acceptably with reverence and godly fear" (Hebrews 12:28).

SEPTEMBER 25, 2022

FAITH INSPIRES GRATITUDE

HEBREWS 12:18–29

Use with Bible Study Guide 4.

WORDS, PHRASES, AND DEFINITIONS

Define or identify.

1. eschatology: ______________________________
2. *ekklesia*: ______________________________
3. "God's wrath": ______________________________
4. innumerable: ______________________________
5. mediator: ______________________________
6. Mosaic Covenant: ______________________________
7. Mount Sinai: ______________________________
8. Mount Zion: ______________________________
9. New Covenant: ______________________________
10. Septuagint: ______________________________

JUMP-STARTING THE LESSON

11. In the In Focus story, how did Warren encourage Lamar, after he had suffered a stroke?

____

____

____

12. According to the In Focus story, God is both ____________________ and ____________________.

UNDERSTANDING THE LESSON

13. From which ethnic group was the majority of the earliest believers in Christ (see Background)? __________

____

14. Believers' names are recorded in Heaven by ____________________; they are written in the ____________________ Book of ____________________ (Hebrews 12:22–23, In Depth).

15. Who is the Mediator or "go-between" between God and sinful humanity (Hebrews 12:24, In Depth, More Light on the Text)? ____

16. In reference to humanity's salvation, what does Jesus' blood do (Hebrews 12:24, More Light on the Text)?

____

____

____

17. Today, God still judges ____________________ (Hebrews 12:25–26, In Depth, More Light on the Text).

18. What are the appropriate responses to the gift we have received (God's great salvation) (Hebrews 12:25–29, In Depth, More Light on the Text)?

a. ____

b. ____

COMMITTING TO THE WORD

19. Memorize and write Hebrews 12:25 verbatim.

____

____

____

WALKING IN THE WORD

20. Write a prayer ***expressing gratitude to God*** for God's wonderful and great salvation.

____

____

____

"And now abideth faith, hope, charity, these three; but the greatest of these is charity" (1 Corinthians 13:13).

OCTOBER 2, 2022

FAITH REQUIRES MUTUAL LOVE

HEBREWS 13:1–3; 1 CORINTHIANS 13

Use with Bible Study Guide 5.

WORDS, PHRASES, AND DEFINITIONS

Match the words, phrases, or names with the correct definitions.

1. _____ "agape love"	a. love of strangers
2. _____ "brotherly love"	b. supernatural language by which a believer communicates with God
3. _____ covetousness	c. arrogant and self-focused; someone who has a "big head"
4. _____ envy	d. sin; personal failures
5. _____ *eros*	e. mutual love; friendship
6. _____ *glossa*	f. the sensuous or erotic form of love
7. _____ hospitality	g. consumed with greed and pursuing selfish desires
8. _____ iniquity	h. jealousy
9. _____ "puffed up"	i. languages
10. _____ tongues	j. a deliberate and willful decision to treat others with the utmost of care and concern

JUMP-STARTING THE LESSON

11. Why was Joyce's pastor concerned about her Christian service (see In Focus)?

____

____

12. Working on other believers' behalf is fine, but it is meaningless unless motivated by what (see In Focus)?

____

____

UNDERSTANDING THE LESSON

13. Because of Christ's ____________________, we are capable of loving others in a deeper and more spiritual way (Hebrews 13:1–3, In Depth).

14. "Let brotherly love continue" is a request (Hebrews 13:1, In Depth, More Light on the Text).

    True False

15. Paul taught in 1 Corinthians 13:1–4 that the gifts were meaningless without love (In Depth, More Light on the Text). True False

16. Explain the phrase "Love is not easily provoked" (1 Corinthians 13:5, In Depth, More Light on the Text).

    ____

    ____

17. True love will produce ____________________, ____________________, and ____________________ (1 Corinthians 13:8–13, In Depth, More Light on the Text).

18. Apostle Paul wanted the Corinthian church to know that giftedness is not the measure of ____________________; the display of ____________________ is (1 Corinthians 13:9–13, In Depth, More Light on the Text).

COMMITTING TO THE WORD

19. a. Memorize and write 1 Corinthians 13:3 verbatim.

    ____

    ____

    b. Explain the meaning of 1 Corinthians 13:3.

    ____

    ____

    ____

WALKING IN THE WORD

20. Share a time when you gave or received love and expected nothing in return.

    ____

    ____

    ____

"And Stephen, full of faith and power, did great wonders and miracles among the people" (Acts 6:8).

OCTOBER 9, 2022

STEPHEN'S ARREST AND SPEECH

ACTS 6:8–7:2a

Use with Bible Study Guide 6.

WORDS, PHRASES, AND DEFINITIONS

Match the words, phrases, or names with the correct definitions.

1. _____ Aramaic	a. the religious council that tried Jesus and Stephen
2. _____ blasphemy	b. the educated people of the Roman Empire spoke this language
3. _____ Cyrene	c. where Paul was born
4. _____ faith	d. an unmerited gift from God
5. _____ grace	e. the language that most Jews in the Holy Land spoke
6. _____ Greek	f. moral conviction; reliance upon Christ
7. _____ Sanhedrin	g. modern day Libya in northern Africa
8. _____ suborned	h. the Church
9. _____ Tarsus	i. bribed; introduced by collusion
10. _____ "The Body of Christ"	j. a disrespectful attitude that finds expression in an act directed against the character of God

JUMP-STARTING THE LESSON

11. Stephen was able to witness with great ________________________ and ________________________ (see the In Focus story).

UNDERSTANDING THE LESSON

12. Besides Stephen, name two other prominent men among the pious Greek-speaking Jews who attended the Synagogue of Libertines or Freedmen (see The People, Places, and Times).

a. ________________________________ b. ________________________________

13. What problem arose between the Aramaic- and the Greek-speaking Jewish Christians (see Background)?

____

____

14. What godly solution did the apostles use to remedy the problem (see Background)?

____

____

15. What were the oppositions to Stephen's actions as a deacon (Acts 6:11–14, In Depth, More Light on the Text)?

a. ____

b. ____

16. Why did Stephen's detractors resort to a smear campaign against him (Acts 6:11, More Light on the Text)?

____

____

17. What did Stephen show through his words and ministry (Acts 6:15, In Depth, More Light on the Text)?

____

____

18. All the rituals of the Old Testament have been superseded by the ____________________ and ____________________ of Jesus (Acts 6:15, In Depth, More Light on the Text).

COMMITTING TO THE WORD

19. Fill in the blanks.

"And Stephen, ____________________ of ____________________ and ____________________, did great ____________________ and ____________________ among the people" (Acts 6:8).

WALKING IN THE WORD

20. Have you ever had someone challenge your Christian witness, or have you ever challenged someone else's? Share below.

____

____

____

____

"And they stoned Stephen, calling upon God, and saying, Lord Jesus, receive my spirit" (Acts 7:59).

STEPHEN'S MARTYRDOM

ACTS 7:51–8:1a

Use with Bible Study Guide 7.

WORDS, PHRASES, AND DEFINITIONS

Define or identify.

1. Abram (Abraham): ________________________________
2. blasphemy: ________________________________
3. "miraculous signs": ________________________________
4. Moses: ________________________________
5. Saul: ________________________________
6. "Son of Man": ________________________________
7. Stephen: ________________________________
8. "stiff-necked": ________________________________
9. "uncircumcised heart": ________________________________
10. witnesses: ________________________________

JUMP-STARTING THE LESSON

11. Sometimes even a life full of goodness and a wise witness will not convince people of the saving grace of God (see In Focus story). True False

UNDERSTANDING THE LESSON

12. Stephen's speech began with a brilliant defense of what he believed was a review of the ____________________ of the people of ____________________ (Acts 7:51–53, In Depth, More Light on the Text).

13. List three accusations that Stephen made against his detractors (Acts 7:51, In Depth, More Light on the Text).

a. ______________________________

b. ______________________________

c. ______________________________

14. How did the prophet Isaiah die (Acts 7:52, More Light on the Text)?

____

____

15. How did the prophet Jeremiah die (Acts 7:52, More Light on the Text)?

____

____

16. All Jews participated in the crucifixion of our Lord (Acts 7:52, More Light on the Text).

True False

17. As they stoned Stephen, he called upon ________________ (Acts 7:59, In Depth, More Light on the Text).

18. At the time of Stephen's death, what was Paul doing (Acts 8:1, In Depth, More Light on the Text)?

____

____

____

COMMITTING TO THE WORD

19. Memorize and write Acts 7:55–56 verbatim.

____

____

____

WALKING IN THE WORD

20. Are you ready to speak up for your Savior, no matter what the consequences in your life will be? Why? Why not?

____

____

____

"And when Simon saw that through laying on of the apostles' hands the Holy Ghost was given, he offered them money" (Acts 8:18).

SIMON WANTS TO BUY POWER

ACTS 8:9–24

Use with Bible Study Guide 8.

STATEMENTS

Explain the meaning.

1. "It is clearly through the power of the Holy Spirit that the men and women of God are able to testify that Jesus is the Christ": ______________________________

____

2. "Miracles clearly point to God, while magic manipulates and points away from God": ______________

____

3. "The miracles that Philip performed aided—not caused—the Samaritans' faith": ______________

____

4. "The fact that the apostles 'laid hands' on the Samaritan converts is no evidence that this was the only way for the Samaritans to receive the Holy Spirit": ______________________________

____

5. "All wrong actions are rooted in the attitudes of the heart": ______________________________

____

6. "Everything we have is a gift from God": ______________________________

____

JUMP-STARTING THE LESSON

7. According to the In Focus story, why did Mr. Jones think that he would be easily elected to his favorite committee: missions? ______________________________

____

8. Do churches ever favor the richer people in the congregation? Why? Why not? ______________________

____

UNDERSTANDING THE LESSON

9. The book of Acts is a book of ____________________ and ____________________; Luke (the writer) provides us with facts of how ____________________ began and spread (see Background).

10. Because of ____________________ witness, many came to ____________________ (Acts 8:9–11, In Depth, More Light on the Text).

11. What two things did Philip preach (Acts 8:12, More Light on the Text)?

    a. ____

    b. ____

12. When the apostles heard that the Samaritans had received the Word of God, why did they send Peter and John to Samaria (Acts 8:14, More Light on the Text)?

    a. ____

    b. ____

13. To be saved, a person must have the ____________________ ____________________ (Acts 8:16, In Depth, More Light on the Text).

14. Define the word "simony" (Acts 8:20, More Light on the Text). ______________________

____

COMMITTING TO THE WORD

15. Memorize and write verbatim Acts 8:20–21.

____

____

____

WALKING IN THE WORD

16. Share some of your motives for following Christ.

____

____

____

"And as they went on their way, they came unto a certain water: and the eunuch said, See, here is water; what doth hinder me to be baptized?" (Acts 8:36)

OCTOBER 30, 2022

PHILIP AND THE ETHIOPIAN EUNUCH

ACTS 8:26–39

Use with Bible Study Guide 9.

WORDS, PHRASES, AND DEFINITIONS

Match the words, phrases, or names with the correct definitions.

1. _____ Candace	a. leading in righteousness or wisdom
2. _____ Esaias	b. an elected deacon in the Jerusalem church
3. _____ Ethiopia	c. a Gentile who had converted to Judaism
4. _____ eunuch	d. queen of the Ethiopians
5. _____ Gaza	e. a state officer; high position in the Ethiopian government
6. _____ guide	f. Isaiah, an Old Testament prophet
7. _____ Philip	g. believing on the Lord Jesus Christ as one's personal Savior
8. _____ proselyte	h. a caravan route leading to Egypt
9. _____ "saving faith"	i. seeking the truth (God's truth)
10. _____ "sincere faith"	j. bordered Egypt to the south of Israel and was known in the Bible as the ancient land of Cush

JUMP-STARTING THE LESSON

11. Philip used the Scriptures to explain salvation to the ________________________

________________________ (see the In Focus story).

UNDERSTANDING THE LESSON

12. One way that God adds to His church is through ________________________ and

________________________ preaching (see Background).

13. Philip's witnessing fulfilled ***Jesus' Great Commission*** to spread the Gospel from ______________________ into ______________________ and ______________________ and to the ______________________ ______________________ of the ______________________ (Ethiopia) (see Background).

14. Philip, under the direction of the ______________________ ______________________, had preached ______________________, which led to the conversion of the ______________________ (Acts 8:26–29, In Depth, More Light on the Text).

COMMITTING TO THE WORD

15. Philip was outstanding in the area of ______________________ (Acts 8:26–29, In Depth, More Light on the Text).

16. ______________________ and the ______________________ of ______________________ must have been integral parts of Philip's life (Acts 8:26–29, In Depth).

17. ______________________ is directly guiding Philip (Acts 8:28–30, More Light on the Text).

18. a. The Scripture in Isaiah that the eunuch read focused on the ______________________ and ______________________ of the Messiah (Acts 8:35, More Light on the Text).

    b. Explain what the above statement means.

    ____

    ____

    ____

19. Fill in the blanks.

    "And Philip said, If thou ______________________ with ______________________ ______________________ ______________________, thou mayest (be baptized). And he answered and said, ______________________ ______________________ that ______________________ ______________________ is the ______________________ of ______________________" (Acts 8:37).

WALKING IN THE WORD

20. Share how you came to a ***saving faith in Jesus Christ***. If you do not yet believe, why not?

    ____

    ____

    ____

"But he said, I am not mad, most noble Festus; but speak forth the words of truth and soberness" (Acts 26:25).

NOVEMBER 6, 2022

PAUL BEFORE KING AGRIPPA

ACTS 26:19–32

Use with Bible Study Guide 10.

WORDS, PHRASES, AND DEFINITIONS

Match the words, phrases, or names with the correct definitions.

1. _____ Agrippa II
2. _____ Ananias
3. _____ Bernice
4. _____ Caesarea Philippi
5. _____ Felix
6. _____ Festus
7. _____ Paul
8. _____ Pharisee
9. _____ repent
10. _____ "shew light"

a. to be sorry for sin and "turn to God"
b. Agrippa's capital
c. Paul had lived as one of these
d. an apostle who helped spread Christianity
e. to make something clear to a wide audience or area
f. He was sent to welcome Paul into the Christian family.
g. Agrippa's sister who lived in an incestuous relationship with him
h. the Jewish governor
i. the new overseer of most of Palestine
j. the great-grandson of Herod the Great who attempted to kill Jesus at birth

JUMP-STARTING THE LESSON

11. Taking a stand for what you believe is ____________________ easy (see In Focus story).

12. God understands that His people are objects of ____________________ and that He can ________________ us to take a ________________ in ________________ name (see In Focus story).

UNDERSTANDING THE LESSON

13. King Agrippa II's power was limited to authority over ____________________ affairs (see The People, Places, and Times).

14. Opposition to Paul often came from the ____________________ who believed he was a ____________________ (see Background).

15. List four accusations brought by the Jews against Paul (see Background):

a. ______________________________ b. ______________________________

c. ______________________________ d. ______________________________

16. According to Paul, what are the Bible's three most important definitions of true repentance and conversion (Acts 26:19–20, More Light on the Text)?

a. ______________________________

b. ______________________________

c. ______________________________

17. Give two examples of evidence of God's help that Paul used in his defense before his accusers (Acts 26:22–23, More Light on the Text).

a. ______________________________

b. ______________________________

18. Paul found the opportunity to share the message of God's revelation through the ____________________, ____________________, and ____________________ of Christ (Acts 26:30–32, More Light on the Text).

COMMITTING TO THE WORD

19. Fill in the blanks.

"Having therefore obtained ____________________ of ____________________, I ____________________ unto this day, ____________________ both to ____________________ and ____________________, saying none other things than those which the ____________________ and ____________________ did say should come: That ____________________ should ____________________, and that he should be the ____________________ that should ____________________ from the ____________________, and should ____________________ ____________________ unto the people, and to the ____________________" (Acts 26:22–23).

WALKING IN THE WORD

20. Share a time when God gave you holy boldness and provided an opportunity for you to declare your Christianity appropriately, articulately, and with love.

____

____

"And the rest, some on boards, and some on broken pieces of the ship. And so it came to pass, that they escaped all safe to land" (Acts 27:44).

NOVEMBER 13, 2022

PAUL SAILS FOR ROME

ACTS 27:1–2, 33–44

Use with Bible Study Guide 11.

WORDS, PHRASES, AND DEFINITIONS

Define or identify.

1. Adramyttium: ____________________
2. Aristarchus: ____________________
3. Caesarea: ____________________
4. delivered: ____________________
5. fasting: ____________________
6. health: ____________________
7. Julius: ____________________
8. Luke: ____________________
9. meat: ____________________
10. willing: ____________________

JUMP-STARTING THE LESSON

11. According to the In Focus story, what enabled Drew to respond to his life storm with cheerfulness, not bitterness? ____________________

____

12. How we weather storms reflects whether we truly have ____________ in God's ____________ (see In Focus story).

UNDERSTANDING THE LESSON

13. Paul exercised his right as a Roman citizen and requested a trial before ____________ (see Background).

14. What did an angel tell Paul about his voyage to Rome (see Background)? ______________________

____

15. List four previously developed, surefire methods that Paul learned in weathering life's storms (Acts 27:33–38, In Depth).

a. ______________________ b. ______________________

c. ______________________ d. ______________________

16. How long were Paul and the other seafarers on board the ship (Acts 27:35, More Light on the Text)?

a. one day b. five days c. one week d. two weeks

17. When the soldiers helping Julius guard the prisoners foresaw the coming destruction of the ship, what did they plan to do to the prisoners (Acts 27:42–44, More Light on the Text)?

____

____

____

18. Other passengers like the centurion observed that Paul faced deadly peril and treated others kindly, which gave witness to the ______________ and ______________ of Paul's ______________ (Acts 27:42–44, More Light on the Text).

COMMITTING TO THE WORD

19. Fill in the blanks.

"And when [Paul] had thus spoken, he took some ______________, and ______________ ______________ to ______________ in the ______________ of them ______________: and when he had broken it, he began to eat. Then they were ______________ ______________ of ______________ ______________, and they also took some meat" (Acts 27:35–36).

WALKING IN THE WORD

20. Share a time when you gave a positive witness of God's goodness in your time of storm.

____

____

____

____

"And it came to pass, that the father of Publius lay sick of a fever and of a bloody flux: to whom Paul entered in, and prayed, and laid his hands on him, and healed him" (Acts 28:8).

NOVEMBER 20, 2022

PAUL MINISTERS IN MALTA

ACTS 28:1–10

Use with Bible Study Guide 12.

WORDS, PHRASES, AND DEFINITIONS

Define or identify.

1. barbarous: ____________________
2. Dike: ____________________
3. flux: ____________________
4. "good Samaritans": ____________________
5. "making God's love real in action": ____________________
6. minister: ____________________
7. Malta: ____________________
8. "philanthropia": ____________________
9. Publius: ____________________
10. Zeus: ____________________

JUMP-STARTING THE LESSON

11. Helping one another becomes easier as we realize ____________________ will often send ____________________ ____________________ to us in our times of need (see the In Focus story).

UNDERSTANDING THE LESSON

12. When the islanders witnessed the snake biting Paul, what did they believe (see Background)?

____

____

____

13. Believers must learn to receive help during difficult situations (Acts 28:1–2, In Depth, More Light on the Text).

True False

14. During stormy seasons of life, we learn there are only small blessings (Acts 28:1–2, In Depth).

True False

15. After the snakebite, what did the Maltese natives expect would happen to Paul (Acts 28:5–6, In Depth, More Light on the Text)? ____

____

16. All people without Christ are bad people (Acts 28:7–8, More Light on the Text).

True False

17. What are two important lessons from the Acts 28 account of Paul's experience on the Island of Malta (Acts 28:9–10, More Light on the Text)?

a. ____

b. ____

18. By making God's love real in action, we can add convicting power to what we say about God's love in Christ (Acts 28:9–10, More Light on the Text).

True False

COMMITTING TO THE WORD

19. Fill in the blanks.

"And it came to pass, that the father of ______________ lay ______________ of a ______________ and of a ______________ ______________: to whom ______________ entered in, and ______________, and ______________ his ______________ on him, and ______________ him. So when this was done, others also, which had ______________ in the island, ______________, and were ______________" (Acts 28:8–9).

WALKING IN THE WORD

20. Share a time when you made God's love real in action for someone in need or someone else made God's love real in action for you.

____

____

"Be it known therefore unto you, that the salvation of God is sent unto the Gentiles, and that they will hear it" (Acts 28:28).

NOVEMBER 27, 2022

PAUL EVANGELIZES IN ROME

ACTS 28:23–31

Use with Bible Study Guide 13.

WORDS, PHRASES, AND DEFINITIONS

Match the words, phrases, or names with the correct definitions.

1.	_____ Caesarea	a. to prevail upon; win over
2.	_____ expound	b. a Roman official
3.	_____ Israel	c. rescue; safety; deliverance
4.	_____ Jerusalem	d. to set forth (used in explaining the way of God)
5.	_____ Messiah	e. mutual questioning; discussion
6.	_____ Pentecost	f. where the Gospel was first to be shared
7.	_____ persuade	g. Jesus would come from here and bring hope to the world.
8.	_____ Porcius Festus	h. Jesus Christ
9.	_____ reasoning	i. Jews who had come to faith started the Roman church during this time.
10.	_____ salvation	j. where Paul's journey started on his way to Rome

JUMP-STARTING THE LESSON

11. Paul is ____________________ but keeps his ____________________ to share the ____________________, which leads to souls coming to ____________________ (see In Focus story).

UNDERSTANDING THE LESSON

12. Why did Paul address the Roman Jewish leaders as "my brothers" (see Background)?

____

____

13. How did Paul explain the fact that he was bound (see Background)?

____

____

14. Paul testified and taught the Jewish leaders about the ____________________ of ____________________ all day into the evening (Acts 28:23–25a, In Depth, More Light on the Text).

15. It was foreordained that the majority of the Jews would not accept their Messiah (Jesus Christ) (Acts 28:25b–27, In Depth).

True False

16. Paul preached to the Jewish people for how many years (Acts 28:25, More Light on the Text)?

a. 1 b. 10 c. 30 d. 40 e. 50

17. Explain what Paul meant by the statement that Gentiles were "grafted in" to God's salvation plan (Acts 28:28, In Depth, More Light on the Text).

____

____

18. Why were some of the Jews rejected in God's salvation plan (Acts 28:28, More Light on the Text)?

____

____

COMMITTING TO THE WORD

19. Memorize and write Acts 28:28 verbatim.

____

____

____

WALKING IN THE WORD

20. What does it mean to you that you were grafted in to God's salvation plan? If you have not yet accepted Jesus Christ as your Lord and Savior, why not?

____

____

____

____

"*Having predestinated us unto the adoption of children by Jesus Christ to himself, according to the good pleasure of his will, To the praise of the glory of his grace, wherein he hath made us accepted in the beloved*" (*Ephesians 1:5–6*).

DECEMBER 4, 2022

SPIRITUAL BLESSINGS IN JESUS CHRIST

EPHESIANS 1:3–14

Use with Bible Study Guide 1.

WORDS, PHRASES, AND DEFINITIONS

Write the definition of the following words.

1. chosen: ______________________________
2. dispensation: ______________________________
3. forgiveness: ______________________________
4. glory: ______________________________
5. "God's incredible grace": ______________________________
6. holy: ______________________________
7. praise: ______________________________
8. predestinated: ______________________________
9. redemption: ______________________________
10. sealed: ______________________________

JUMP-STARTING THE LESSON

11. Describe the child that Regina and Aaron adopted (see the In Focus story).

____

____

____

12. God provided a way ***to adopt*** us into His family— ____________ through His ____________, ____________ ____________ (see the In Focus story).

UNDERSTANDING THE LESSON

13. Paul ***wrote the book of Ephesians*** perhaps while he was imprisoned in ____________________ (see The People, Places, and Times).

14. The ***vast plan of redemption*** covers what period of time (see Background)?

____

____

15. God ____________________, ____________________, and ____________________ ***our redemption***, not because of any ____________________ or ____________________; but because He is ____________________ and. ____________________ (Ephesians 1:3–5, In Depth).

16. Why does the apostle Paul ***praise and bless God*** (Ephesians 1:3–6, In Depth, More Light on the Text)?

____

____

17. What is a "biblical mystery" (Ephesians 1:9, More Light on the Text)?

____

____

18. The experience of salvation comes from ____________________ the ____________________ of ____________________ (Ephesians 1:13, More Light on the Text).

COMMITTING TO THE WORD

19. Memorize and write Ephesians 1:4–5 verbatim.

____

____

____

WALKING IN THE WORD

20. On the lines below, express ***your appreciation*** for God choosing you to become a part of His family.

____

____

____

"In whom all the building fitly framed together groweth unto an holy temple in the Lord" (Ephesians 2:21).

DECEMBER 11, 2022

ONE IN JESUS CHRIST

EPHESIANS 2:11–22

Use with Bible Study Guide 2.

WORDS, PHRASES, AND DEFINITIONS

Match the words, phrases, or names with the correct definitions.

1. _____ abolished	a. citizenship within the community
2. _____ access	b. non-Jewish nations by birth
3. _____ "chief cornerstone"	c. describes how separated the Gentiles were from Christ
4. _____ circumcision	d. done away with, rendered idle, or destroyed
5. _____ commonwealth	e. one who lives in a place without the right of citizenship
6. _____ "far off"	f. being built into a spiritual house to be a holy priesthood
7. _____ "Holy of Holies"	g. the act of removing the foreskin of the male sex organ
8. _____ "living stones"	h. He joins two walls (Jews/Gentiles) that were once separated.
9. _____ strangers	i. the inner court of the temple; the place where God dwelled
10. _____ uncircumcised	j. the freedom believers have to approach God as our Father with boldness and assurance that we are acceptable to Him and that we shall not be turned down

JUMP-STARTING THE LESSON

11. Paul tackled ***the problem of division*** between the ____________________ and ____________________ in the ____________________ congregation (see In Focus story).

UNDERSTANDING THE LESSON

12. In the Jewish Temple, where did ***Gentiles*** have to stay (see The People, Places, and Times)?

____

____

13. When Jesus was crucified, what happened to ***the curtain*** of the "Holy of Holies" (see The People, Places, and Times)?

____

____

14. Because many barriers divided the Jews and the Gentiles in the ancient world, ***Paul devoted much of his attention*** in his letter to the Ephesians to the essential ___________________ of the ___________________ (see Background).

15. Even though Isaiah foretold that the blessing would flow to all nations, the Messiah was promised to the Jews, ***not*** the Gentiles (Ephesians 2:11–13, In Depth). True False

16. To make ***the unification of Jews and Gentiles clear***, apostle Paul declared in Ephesians 2:14 that ***"He is our peace."*** Who was he speaking of, and what is one of His titles (More Light on the Text)?

____

____

17. The unification of ***all*** believers (the church) in Christ includes the abolition of the ___________________, ___________________, and ___________________ distinctions (Ephesians 2:15, More Light on the Text).

18. List three things, according to apostle Paul, that Christ has done through His blood to bring about unification in the body of Christ (Ephesians 2:16–17, More Light on the Text).

a. ____

b. ____

c. ____

COMMITTING TO THE WORD

19. Memorize and write Ephesians 2:14–17 verbatim.

____

____

____

WALKING IN THE WORD

20. What can ***you do to help promote peace and unity*** in your church?

____

____

____

"There is one body, and one Spirit, even as ye are called in one hope of your calling; One Lord, one faith, one baptism" (Ephesians 4:4–5).

DECEMBER 18, 2022

UNITY IN THE BODY OF CHRIST

EPHESIANS 4:1–16

Use with Bible Study Guide 3.

WORDS, PHRASES, AND DEFINITIONS

Define or identify.

1. apostle: ____________________
2. edify: ____________________
3. evangelist: ____________________
4. forbearing: ____________________
5. "lowliness of mind": ____________________
6. meekness: ____________________
7. prophets: ____________________
8. "spiritual gifts": ____________________
9. vocation: ____________________
10. "walk worthy": ____________________

JUMP-STARTING THE LESSON

11. How can ***Aaron and the other younger church members*** use their spiritual gifts to help build up their church (see the In Focus story)? ____________________
12. Although each church has its problems, what are ***some of the ways you can use your gifts to build up*** your church (see the In Focus story)? ____________________

UNDERSTANDING THE LESSON

13. ***Every believer*** has a spiritual gift (see The People, Places, and Times). True False
14. Spiritual gifts are ***just*** for individual benefit or pleasure (see The People, Places, and Times). True False

15. The ***greatest gift***, which Paul said every believer should possess, is ____________________ (see The People, Places, and Times).

16. A ***healthy formula for keeping the unity*** in the body of Christ is threefold (Ephesians 4:1–6, In Depth):

a. ____________________

b. ____________________

c. ____________________

17. Explain how, according to apostle Paul, the unity of the Church arises from the unity of the Godhead—the Father, Son, and Holy Spirit (Ephesians 4:4, More Light on the Text).

____

____

18. ***According to Apostle Paul***, ____________________ and ____________________ are essential in the life of the body of Christ (Ephesians 4:15, More Light on the Text).

COMMITTING TO THE WORD

19. Fill in the blanks.

"Endeavouring to keep the ____________________ of the ____________________ in the ____________________ of ____________________. There is ____________________ ____________________, and ____________________ ____________________, even as ye are called in ____________________ ____________________ of your calling; ____________________ ____________________, ____________________ ____________________, ____________________ ____________________, ____________________ ____________________ and ____________________ of ____________________, who is above ____________________, and through ____________________, and in you. But unto ____________________ ____________________ of us is given ____________________ according to the measure of the ____________________ of ____________________" (Ephesians 4:3–7).

WALKING IN THE WORD

20. Share ***what you can do to enhance*** your spiritual growth.

____

____

____

____

"And Mary said, My soul doth magnify the Lord, And my spirit hath rejoiced in God my Saviour" (Luke 1:46–47)

ACCORDING TO THE PROMISE

LUKE 1:46–55

Use with Bible Study Guide 4.

WORDS, PHRASES, AND DEFINITIONS

Define or identify.

1. angels: ____________________
2. Elizabeth: ____________________
3. Gabriel: ____________________
4. "handmaiden": ____________________
5. immutable: ____________________
6. John the Baptist: ____________________
7. "Magnificat": ____________________
8. "magnify": ____________________
9. soul: ____________________
10. strophes: ____________________

JUMP-STARTING THE LESSON

11. In the In Focus story, Michelle showed Brenda that God is always ____________________ and ____________________, even in very rough situations.

UNDERSTANDING THE LESSON

12. The ____________________ and ____________________ never leave the immediate presence of God and are worshiping Him continually (see The People, Places, and Times).
13. Approximately how old was Mary when she was pregnant with Jesus (see Background)?

    a. 12 b. 15 c. 20 d. 25 e. 30 f. 40

14. List the three strophes (stanzas) that Mary's song of praise (the Magnificat) can be divided into (see Introduction of More Light on the Text).

a. ____________________

b. ____________________

c. ____________________

15. In her "song of praise," Mary recognized that God had looked upon her with ____________________ and had given her a place of ____________________ (Luke 1:48, More Light on the Text).

16. List three attributes of God that Mary acknowledges in Luke 1:49 (More Light on the Text). His:

a. ______________ b. ______________ c. ______________

17. What attribute of God does Mary acknowledge in Luke 1:50 (In Depth, More Light on the Text)?

____

____

18. In Luke 1:54–55, through the incarnation of Christ (His coming to earth as the God-Man), what five attributes should we realize (More Light on the Text)? His:

a. ______________ b. ______________

c. ______________ d. ______________

e. ______________

COMMITTING TO THE WORD

19. Memorize and write Luke 1:46–48 verbatim.

____

____

____

____

WALKING IN THE WORD

20. Write your own "Magnificat" (song or hymn of praise) of what God has done in your life.

____

____

____

____

"Submitting yourselves one to another in the fear of God" (Ephesians 5:21).

JANUARY 1, 2023

CHRIST'S LOVE FOR THE CHURCH

EPHESIANS 5:21–6:4

Use with Bible Study Guide 5.

WORDS, PHRASES, AND DEFINITIONS

Match the words, phrases, or names with the correct definitions.

1. _____ "Household Code"
2. _____ "self-sacrificing love"
3. _____ head
4. _____ "live wisely"
5. _____ nourisheth
6. _____ "nurture and admonition of the Lord"
7. _____ obey
8. _____ provoke
9. _____ respect
10. _____ submit

a. to rouse to wrath; exasperate; anger
b. to be led by the Spirit
c. what husbands and wives should exercise toward each other
d. to raise children according to God's principles
e. standards of how the father should lead his family
f. an unselfish love
g. a voluntary attitude of cooperating
h. portraying leadership
i. providing sustenance for others
j. how children should act toward their parents

JUMP-STARTING THE LESSON

11. What did Angie ***do after*** reading her students' papers about what they wished (see In Focus Story)?

____

____

12. Angie knew that ***her students needed*** the ____________________ of ____________________ to permeate their lives and ____________________ their families (see In Focus).

UNDERSTANDING THE LESSON

13. When we are ***living a Spirit-led life***, God gives us the ________________ to live in an attitude of ________________ and ________________ to others (Ephesians 5:21–24, In Depth).

14. Whenever there is a ***true submission*** for the sake of the Lord, it leads to a frame of ________________ and an ________________ that is penetrated with a deep sense of ________________ (Ephesians 5:21–24, More Light on the Text).

15. ***God ordained*** the husband as ________________ ________________ ________________ ________________ (see Ephesians 5:21–24, More Light on the Text).

16. Christ's ***love for the church*** was ________________ - ________________ (Ephesians 5:25–33, In Depth).

17. The word ***cherisheth*** refers to a husband's promise to his wife to, ________________, and shelter her ________________, ________________, ________________, and ________________ in all situations (Ephesians 5:29, More Light on the Text).

18. Apostle Paul was ***admonishing*** the husband to "________________ his wife" and the wife to "see that she ________________ her husband" (Ephesians 5:33, More Light on the Text).

COMMITTING TO THE WORD

19. a. Memorize and write Ephesians 5:22 and 25 verbatim.

____

____

____

b. Explain their meanings:

____

____

____

WALKING IN THE WORD

20. Why should you as a believer ***submit*** to other believers?

____

____

____

"What then? notwithstanding, every way, whether in pretence, or in truth, Christ is preached; and I therein do rejoice, yea, and will rejoice" (Philippians 1:18).

PROCLAIMING CHRIST

PHILIPPIANS 1:15–26

Use with Bible Study Guide 6.

WORDS, PHRASES, AND DEFINITIONS

Match the words, phrases, or names with the correct definitions.

1. _____ Claudius	a. rivalry; wrangling
2. _____ contention	b. It is believed that both Paul and Peter were martyred during his reign.
3. _____ envy	c. selfishness; a desire to put oneself forward
4. _____ Garius	d. of goodwill
5. _____ Jerusalem	e. the Greek translation of the Jewish Scriptures
6. _____ Nero	f. jealousy; ill will
7. _____ "pure motive"	g. He expelled some Jews from Rome because they spread the Gospel.
8. _____ Rome	h. where Paul was imprisoned in a Roman barracks
9. _____ Septuagint	i. emperor of Rome
10. _____ strife	j. where Christianity had been established prior to Paul's coming

JUMP-STARTING THE LESSON

11. During ***his battle with cancer***, what was ***important*** to Warren (see the In Focus story)?

____

____

____

12. As ***we meet the challenges of life***, what are people watching to see in our lives (see In Focus story)?

____

____

____

UNDERSTANDING THE LESSON

13. During the time that the New Testament was written, what were four reasons people could be imprisoned (see The People, Places, and Times)?

    a. ______________________________

    b. ______________________________

    c. ______________________________

    d. ______________________________

14. Even as he sat in prison, ***apostle Paul's letter*** was full of ______________, ______________, and ______________ for those who were carrying on the work of spreading the Gospel (see Background).

15. Some followers were ***stronger*** because Paul was in jail (Philippians 1:15–18, In Depth). True False

16. Paul ***did not feel*** that the Gospel was powerful enough ***to transcend*** human pettiness (Philippians 1:15–18, In Depth). True False

17. Even though apostle Paul was in jail, what were ***two of his convictions*** (Philippians 1:20, More Light on the Text)?

    a. ______________________________

    b. ______________________________

18. Apostle Paul determined ***that regardless of his circumstances***, he would remain ______________ to the end so that Christ's name would be ______________ (Philippians 1:20, More Light on the Text).

COMMITTING TO THE WORD

19. Fill in the blanks.

    "According to my ______________ ______________ and my ______________, that in nothing I shall be ______________, but that with ______________, as always, so now also ______________ shall be ______________ in ______________ ______________, whether it be by ______________, or by ______________. For to me to ______________ is ______________, and to ______________ is ______________" (Philippians 1:20–21).

WALKING IN THE WORD

20. If you were ***told today*** that you may not live much longer, ***what preparation would you make to insure that Christ would be glorified*** through your experience from passing from life to death?

    ____

    ____

“Let this mind be in you, which was also in Christ Jesus” (Philippians 2:5)

JANUARY 15, 2023

JESUS’ HUMILITY AND EXALTATION

PHILIPPIANS 2:5–11

Use with Bible Study Guide 7.

WORDS, PHRASES, AND DEFINITIONS

Define or identify.

1. “*agape* love”: ______________________________
2. Christ came into existence “in the likeness of man”: ______________________________
3. exalted: ______________________________
4. Jesus “being found in fashion as a man”: ______________________________
5. Jesus “made himself of no reputation”: ______________________________
6. Jesus “taking the form of a servant”: ______________________________
7. Philippi:______________________________
8. Romans: ______________________________
9. servant: ______________________________
10. YAHWEH: ______________________________

JUMP-STARTING THE LESSON

11. What did Rev. Williams learn about his church member ***Myrtle Jenkins’ opposition to the new facility*** the church was about to purchase (see In Focus story)? ______________________________

____

12. Paul advises us ***to have*** the ____________________ of ____________________ (see In Focus).

UNDERSTANDING THE LESSON

13. The Philippian church could ***ill afford*** to let ____________________ ____________________ afflict their ____________________ for ____________________ (see Background).

14. Apostle Paul ***appealed to the Philippian church*** for ____________________ and ____________________-
____________________ as exemplified in ____________________ (Philippians 2:5–8, In Depth).

15. To become human, what six things did ***Christ empty Himself of*** (Philippians 2:7, More Light on the Text)?

a. ________________________________,
b. ________________________________,
c. ________________________________,
d. ________________________________,
e. ________________________________,
f. ________________________________

16. Explain the following verses: "Humble yourselves therefore under the mighty hand of God, that he may exalt you in due time" (1 Peter 5:6); "Humble yourselves in the sight of the Lord, and he shall lift you up" (James 4:10; Philippians 2:9–11, In Depth).

____

____

17. What does ***Christ's super-exaltation*** mean (Philippians 2:9, More Light on the Text)?

____

____

18. ***All creation*** that will pay homage to Christ includes:

a. ________________________________,
b. ________________________________,
c. ________________________________,
d. ________________________________,
e. ________________________________,
f. ________________________________

(Philippians 2:10, More Light on the Text)

COMMITTING TO THE WORD

19. Memorize and write Philippians 2:9–11 verbatim.

____

____

____

WALKING IN THE WORD

20. ***Are you willing*** to offer yourself as a sacrifice for the benefit of fellow Christians and those who have yet to come to know Christ? Why? Why not?

____

____

____

"But what things were gain to me, those I counted loss for Christ" (Philippians 3:7).

JANUARY 22, 2023

GAINING IN JESUS CHRIST

PHILIPPIANS 3:7–11

Use with Bible Study Guide 8.

STATEMENTS

Explain the meaning.

1. "Apostle Paul railed against the problem of having confidence in the flesh, versus the knowledge of Christ": ____

2. "Apostle Paul came to realize that ***no legalistic training or adherence*** could save anyone": ____

3. "***To know Christ*** is not merely an intellectual understanding of who He is": ______________________________

4. "The Pharisees were a sect of self-righteous and zealous Jews who ***held to the letters of their interpretation of the law and to their own traditions*** without minding whether they nullified the Word of God or not": ____

5. "Apostle Paul's quest to know Christ ***cost him everything***, including the highest position, which he had attained within Judaism": ____

6. "The ***Pharisaic righteousness*** was self-righteousness": ____

JUMP-STARTING THE LESSON

7. According to the In Focus story, what ***really changed*** Aaron's life? ____

UNDERSTANDING THE LESSON

8. What ***view of life*** did the Libertines hold (see The People, Places, and Times)? ______________________

____

9. List ***four gains*** that Paul counted as loss for Christ's sake (Philippians 3:7–9, In Depth).

a. ____________________ b. ____________________

c. ____________________ d. ____________________

10. In evaluating his past, list ***seven things that apostle Paul saw as worthless*** compared with his new privilege of knowing Christ (Philippians 3:7, More Light on the Text). a. ____________________

b. ____________________ c. ____________________

d. ____________________ e. ____________________

f. ____________________ g. ____________________

11. Apostle Paul's ***surrender*** of ____________ and ____________ – ____________ did not cause him to go to the other extreme of libertinism (Philippians 3:10–11, In Depth).

12. For what ***three reasons*** did apostle Paul say that the resurrection of Jesus Christ is important to us (Philippians 3:10–11, In Depth)?

a. ______________ b. ______________ c. ______________

13. ***Christ's righteousness***, which through His ____________ has been ____________ to all ____________ (Philippians 3:10, More Light on the Text).

14. Apostle Paul ***strives*** to live a life ____________ the ____________ and ____________ of his Savior ____________ (Philippians 3:11, More Light on the Text)?

COMMITTING TO THE WORD

15. Memorize and write verbatim Philippians 3:7–8.

____

____

____

WALKING IN THE WORD

16. What have ***you given up*** to follow Christ?

____

____

"Nevertheless, whereto we have already attained, let us walk by the same rule, let us mind the same thing" (Philippians 3:16).

JANUARY 29, 2023

STAND FIRM

PHILIPPIANS 3:12–16

Use with Bible Study Guide 9.

WORDS, PHRASES, AND DEFINITIONS

Match the words, phrases, or names with the correct definitions.

1. _____ arrived
2. _____ attained
3. _____ "follow after"
4. _____ "I may apprehend"
5. _____ "let us walk"
6. _____ perfect
7. _____ press
8. _____ "reach forth"
9. _____ reveal
10. _____ worry

a. the opposite of trust
b. disclose what before was unknown
c. took hold of; received
d. fulfill; finish; complete a given task; consummate; mature
e. pursue; follow after; work hard; do one's best
f. run swiftly in order to catch a person or thing
g. to have taken hold of the goal; reached the finishing line
h. march in a row or in orderly ranks; conform to the standards
i. obtain; lay hold of
j. stretch oneself

JUMP-STARTING THE LESSON

11. "***I see your knowledge, achievements, and accomplishments but what about your*** ____________________ ____________________ ____________________ ______________ (see the In Focus story)?"

12. Apostle Paul wanted to ***encourage*** the Philippians to ____________________ our ____________________ in their daily lives—stay in the ____________________ (see the In Focus story).

UNDERSTANDING THE LESSON

13. What is the ***major difference*** between the Grecian race and our race in Christ Jesus (see The People, Places, and Times)? ____

14. When the Lord sent Ananias to pray with Paul, after apostle Paul was in Damascus for three days fasting and unable to see, what did the Lord tell ***Ananias that Paul would do for God*** (see Background)?

____

____

COMMITTING TO THE WORD

15. Why did apostle Paul ***not consider*** his past achievements to be sufficient for winning the race; he could not rest on past accomplishments (Philippians 3:12–14, In Depth)?

____

____

16. Salvation ***has both*** a ______________ and an ______________, but it is, a ______________, a ______________ achievement (Philippians 3:12–14, In Depth).

17. What ***three things*** did the apostle Paul do in his focus on the race before him so that he would not be distracted from his bid for the prize (to hear God say, "Well done my good and faithful servant") (Philippians 3:13–14, In Depth, More Light on the Text)?

a. ______________ b. ______________ c. ______________

18. ***Compare and contrast*** an earthly race with the heavenly race (Philippians 3:13–14, More Light on the Text).

a. ______________________________

b. ______________________________

c. ______________________________

19. Fill in the blanks.

"Brethren, I count not myself to have ______________ but this one thing I do,

______________ those things which are ______________, and ______________ forth

unto those things which are ______________, I ______________ ______________

the ______________ for the ______________ of the ______________

______________ of ______________ in Christ Jesus" (Philippians 3:13–14).

WALKING IN THE WORD

20. Share what you ***need to do to commit your life completely*** to Jesus.

____

____

____

"For it pleased the Father that in him should all fulness dwell" (Colossians 1:19).

FEBRUARY 5, 2023

THE SUPREMACY OF JESUS CHRIST

COLOSSIANS 1:15–20

Use with Bible Study Guide 10.

WORDS, PHRASES, AND DEFINITIONS

Match the words, phrases, or names with the correct definitions.

1. _____ "Christ is before all things."	a. likeness or representation
2. _____ firstborn	b. the church
3. _____ fullness	c. to be first in rank, influence, and importance
4. _____ heretics	d. something that completes
5. _____ image	e. the first one to be born into a family
6. _____ "invisible things"	f. cosmic; earthly; material; including humans
7. _____ preeminence	g. false teachers
8. _____ "visible things"	h. Christ created all things.
9. _____ "the agent of all creation"	i. thrones, dominions, principalities, and powers
10. _____ "the body of Christ"	j.Christ is from eternity.

JUMP-STARTING THE LESSON

11. ***How did Brenda*** view her life (see In Focus story)? ______________________________

12. According to the In Focus story, ***what two things*** does the lesson give?

a. ______________________________

b. ______________________________

UNDERSTANDING THE LESSON

13. Colosse is in ***modern-day*** __________________ (see the People, Places, and Times).

14. Who was ***founder*** of the church in Colosse __________________ (see Background)?

15. Creation ***was through*** ____________________ (Colossians 1:15–17, In Depth).

16. Believers ***have redemption*** through Christ's ____________________, even the ____________________ of ____________________ (Colossians 1:14–15, More Light on the Text).

17. Explain the phrase, ***"He (Christ) upholds and sustains all things"*** (Colossians 1:17, More Light on the Text).

____

____

____

18. Explain the phrase, ***Christ is "the firstborn from the dead"*** (Colossians 1:18, More Light on the Text).

____

____

____

COMMITTING TO THE WORD

19. a. Fill in the blanks.

"For by ____________________ were ____________________ things ____________________, that are in ____________________, and that are in ____________________, ____________________ and ____________________, whether they be ____________________, or ____________________, or ____________________, or ____________________: ____________________ things were ____________________ by ____________________, and for ____________________" (Colossians 1:16).

b. Explanation:

____

____

____

WALKING IN THE WORD

20. Write a prayer ***giving thanks*** to Sovereign God for all God has created and done in your life.

____

____

____

____

"And ye are complete in him, which is the head of all principality and power" (Colossians 2:10).

FEBRUARY 12, 2023

FULL LIFE IN CHRIST

COLOSSIANS 2:6–15

Use with Bible Study Guide 11.

WORDS, PHRASES, AND DEFINITIONS

Define or identify.

1. circumcision: ______________________________
2. established: ______________________________
3. fullness: ______________________________
4. Gnosticism: ______________________________
5. Godhead: ______________________________
6. receive: ______________________________
7. rooted: ______________________________
8. "stand firm": ______________________________
9. vain: ______________________________
10. walk: ______________________________

JUMP-STARTING THE LESSON

11. According to the In Focus story, ***what was Tamika's misunderstanding*** about personal salvation?

____

____

12. As believers, we should be ***exhorted and reminded*** of the ______________ we have in ______________ and stay ______________ in the faith (see In Focus).

UNDERSTANDING THE LESSON

13. Jesus was truly ***God in the*** ______________ (see The People, Places, and Times).

14. What problem did ***heretical teaching*** cause in the Colossian church (see Background)?

____

____

15. Paul affirms that ***believers*** have received Christ Jesus as Lord and ***should live*** their lives

______________, ______________, and ______________ in Him alone

(Colossians 2:6–8, In Depth).

16. ***Believers are*** ______________ in Christ (Colossians 2:11–15, In Depth, More Light on the Text).

17. Moses told the people that they ***must be circumcised*** in the ______________ as well as the

______________ (Colossians 2:11, More Light on the Text).

18. Because of Christ's death on the Cross for believers, ***what happened to the record*** of our sins (Colossians 2:13–14, In Depth, More Light on the Text)?

____

____

____

COMMITTING TO THE WORD

19. Fill in the blanks.

"And you, being ______________ in your ______________ and the

______________ of your ______________, hath he quickened together with

him, having ______________ you ______________ ______________;

______________ ______________ the handwriting of ______________ that

was against us, which was contrary to us, and took it out of the way, ______________ it to

______________ ______________" (Colossians 2:13–14).

WALKING IN THE WORD

20. Share ***how you feel*** that Christ's death on the Cross wiped away the record of your sins, just as though you had never sinned.

____

____

____

____

"And above all these things put on charity, which is the bond of perfectness" (Colossians 3:14).

FEBRUARY 19, 2023

CLOTHED WITH CHRIST

COLOSSIANS 3:5–17

Use with Bible Study Guide 12.

WORDS, PHRASES, AND DEFINITIONS

Define or identify.

1. blasphemy: ____________________
2. covetousness: ____________________
3. fornication: ____________________
4. impurity: ____________________
5. longsuffering: ____________________
6. malice: ____________________
7. mortify: ____________________
8. perfectness: ____________________
9. sanctification: ____________________
10. Scythians: ____________________

JUMP-STARTING THE LESSON

11. Apostle Paul is exhorting the church at Colosse to __________ __________ the __________ __________ and put on the __________ __________ ***in Christ***. (see In Focus story)

UNDERSTANDING THE LESSON

12. The apostle Paul says ***we have a new life in Christ*** and the old life is __________ (Colossians 3:5–9, In Depth).

13. Apostle Paul is calling for ***a slaying of*** __________ __________, __________, and __________ that root themselves in our bodies (Colossians 3:5–9, In Depth).

14. Explain what apostle Paul means by ***"put on the new man"*** (Colossians 3:10, More Light on the Text).

____

____

15. Explain what apostle Paul means by the statement ***"Christians are called the 'chosen' or 'elect' of God"*** (Colossians 3:12, More Light on the Text).

____

____

16. Explain what apostle Paul means when he says that believers should strive for the attribute of ***"longsuffering"*** (Colossians 3:12, More Light on the Text).

____

____

17. We should allow the ____________________ of God ***to rule*** in our ____________________ (Colossians 3:15, More Light on the Text).

18. When believers are ***abundantly equipped with all wisdom through the Word of Christ***, we will ____________________ and ____________________ each other gently through ____________________ and ____________________ and ____________________ ____________________ (Colossians 3:16, More Light on the Text).

COMMITTING TO THE WORD

19. Fill in the blanks.

"Put on therefore, as the ____________________ of God, ____________________ and beloved, bowels of ____________________, ____________________, ____________________ ____________________ ____________________, ____________________, ____________________; ____________________ one another, and ____________________ one another, if any man have a quarrel against any: even as Christ forgave you, so also do ye. And above all these things put on ____________________, which is the bond of perfectness" (Colossians 3:12–14).

WALKING IN THE WORD

20. Explain how you have become ***"a new creation" in Christ***, where old things have passed away.

____

____

"And say to Archippus, Take heed to the ministry which thou hast received in the Lord, that thou fulfil it" (Colossians 4:17).

FEBRUARY 26, 2023

SPIRITUAL DISCIPLINES FOR NEW LIFE

COLOSSIANS 4:2–6

Use with Bible Study Guide 13.

WORDS, PHRASES, AND DEFINITIONS

Write the following words' definitions as they relate to today's lesson.

1. _____ continue	a. to give strict attention to
2. _____ Door	b. the act of Christ taking on human flesh
3. _____ epistle	c. direct conversation with God
4. _____ "godly speech"	d. opportunity to witness
5. _____ Incarnation	e. to give unremitting care to a person or thing
6. _____ prayer	f. letter
7. _____ thanksgiving	g. conduct
8. _____ walk	h. behaving in a godly manner
9. _____ watch	i. conversation governed by peace, love, and compassion
10. _____ "wise conduct"	j. an attitude of gratitude, humility, submission, and reverence toward God

JUMP-STARTING THE LESSON

11. Why did ***Felicia begin to feel*** that God had abandoned her (see In Focus story)?

____

____

____

12. ***Practicing spiritual discipline*** is _______________ to our walk with Christ (see In Focus story).

UNDERSTANDING THE LESSON

13. ***Where was apostle Paul*** when he wrote this epistle to the Colossians (see Background)?

____

____

14. In this letter to the Colossians, what ***three things*** did apostle Paul urge them to do (Colossians 4:2–4, In Depth)?

a. _______________

b. _______________

c. _______________

15. Paul wrote that believers ***should "continue*** in _______________" (Colossians 4:2–4, In Depth).

16. ***Our lives are powerful witnesses*** to everyone (Colossians 4:4, More Light on the Text).

True False

17. A faith that ***is worth the sacrifice of one's life isn't worth*** following (Colossians 4:4, More Light on the Text).

True False

18. Christians ***should take advantage*** of every opportunity to display lives influenced by their _______________ (Colossians 4:5–6, In Depth).

COMMITTING TO THE WORD

19. Memorize and write Colossians 4:5–6 verbatim.

____

____

____

____

WALKING IN THE WORD

20. What does ***your prayer life*** look like, and how can you improve it?

____

____

____

____

"And there was given him dominion, and glory, and a kingdom, that all people, nations, and languages, should serve him: his dominion is an everlasting dominion, which shall not pass away, and his kingdom that which shall not be destroyed" (Daniel 7:14).

MARCH 5, 2023

DANIEL'S VISION OF CHANGE

DANIEL 7:9–14

Use with Bible Study Guide 1.

WORDS, PHRASES, AND DEFINITIONS

Write the definition of the following words.

1. beheld: ______________________________
2. Cyrus: ______________________________
3. Darius: ______________________________
4. eschatology: ______________________________
5. horn: ______________________________
6. Nebuchadnezzar: ______________________________
7. sovereignty: ______________________________
8. the "Ancient of Days": ______________________________
9. the"Daniel fast": ______________________________
10. the "Son of man": ______________________________

JUMP-STARTING THE LESSON

11. What did Regina, the bank representative, tell Marcus and Felicia about ***opening a joint account*** (see the In Focus story)? ______________________________

____

____

12. According to In Focus, what did the prophet Daniel's ***dream foreshadow***?

____

____

____

UNDERSTANDING THE LESSON

13. This same ***vision of God as judge*** that was given to Daniel was also given to whom (see The People, Places, and Times)? ____________________

14. By ***his words and actions***, what did Daniel advocate in our relations with God (see The People, Places, and Times and Background)? ____________________

____

____

____

15. ***Daniel's prophecy*** was one of ____________________ (see Background).

16. ***The Ancient of Days*** is a name that characterizes God as a judge whose reign is ____________________ (Daniel 7:9–12, In Depth, More Light on the Text).

17. ____________________ is often used to ***symbolize God*** in the Old Testament (Daniel 7:9, More Light on the Text).

18. In Daniel 7:11–12, what did ***"the boasting mouth of the horn" represent*** (In Depth, More Light on the Text)?

____

____

____

COMMITTING TO THE WORD

19. Memorize and write Daniel 7:14 verbatim.

____

____

____

____

WALKING IN THE WORD

20. Is there something in your life that God is trying to ***get you to see, to change***? If so, discuss on the given lines.

____

____

____

____

"To the Lord our God belong mercies and forgivenesses, though we have rebelled against him" (Daniel 9:9).

DANIEL'S PRAYER

DANIEL 9:4B–14

Use with Bible Study Guide 2.

WORDS, PHRASES, AND DEFINITIONS

Match the words, phrases, or names with the correct definitions.

1. _____ Babylon	a. to go away or depart from the truth or way
2. _____ *elohiym*	b. the angel God used to respond to Daniel's prayer
3. _____ forgivenesses	c. guilt or condemnation
4. _____ Gabriel	d. to commit an unfaithful or treacherous act
5. _____ iniquity	e. pardon
6. _____ Josiah	f. a common reference of "God"
7. _____ Manasseh	g. where the Israelites were held captive for 70 years
8. _____ transgress	h. a king that followed the Lord
9. _____ trespass	i. perverse or perversion
10. _____ wickedness	j. the son of King Hezekiah; he was a wicked king

JUMP-STARTING THE LESSON

11. Why was Tamika ***arrested*** (see In Focus story)? ____

____

____

____

12. ***Why*** did Daniel go to God in prayer (see In Focus)? ________________________________

____

____

____

UNDERSTANDING THE LESSON

13. ***God's judgment on Israel*** came during the reign of what prophet (see Background)?

____

14. With regards to his people, ***what*** was Daniel's concern (Daniel 9:4b–8, In Depth)?

____

15. What ***three things*** did Daniel do to prepare himself for a solemn prayer to the Lord (Daniel 9:4b, More Light on the Text)?

 a. ____

 b. ____

 c. ____

16. ***Daniel's prayer*** has been called a ____________________ of ____________________ Daniel 9:5–6, More Light on the Text).

17. Daniel knew that even when he and his people were not faithful, ***God is continuously*** ____________________ (Daniel 9:9, More Light on the Text).

18. Daniel ***counts himself*** as one of Israel's ____________________ (Daniel 9:12–14, More Light on the Text).

COMMITTING TO THE WORD

19. Memorize and write Daniel 9:9 verbatim.

____

____

____

WALKING IN THE WORD

20. Write your own ***prayer of penitence***.

____

____

____

____

____

____

Amen.

"And the vision of the evening and the morning which was told is true: wherefore shut thou up the vision; for it shall be for many days" (Daniel 8:26).

MARCH 19, 2023

GABRIEL'S INTERPRETATION

DANIEL 8:19–26

Use with Bible Study Guide 3.

WORDS, PHRASES, AND DEFINITIONS

Write the following words' definitions as relates to today's lesson.

1. "after many days": ______
2. Antiochus Epiphanes: ______
3. epiphany: ______
4. eschatology: ______
5. Gabriel: ______
6. indignation: ______
7. "the animals": ______
8. "the indignation": ______
9. "the ram": ______
10. "the two horns": ______

JUMP-STARTING THE LESSON

11. In the In Focus story, what was ***Andre ashamed*** of? ______

12. What was Anthony's ***final advice*** to Andre, his old friend (see the In Focus story)? ______

UNDERSTANDING THE LESSON

13. Daniel's vision was about what ***three*** things (see Background)?

    a. ____________________

    b. ____________________

    c. ____________________

14. Daniel's vision was ***a vision of*** ____________________ for those who live in calamitous times, knowing that there should be an end to them (Daniel 8:19–22, In Depth).

15. According to the vision, Antiochus set himself against what ***three*** things (Daniel 8:23–26, In Depth)?

    a. ____________________

    b. ____________________

    c. ____________________

16. Epiphanes ***blasphemously*** called himself ____________________, while others called him Epimanes, which means ____________________ (Daniel 8:23–24, More Light on the Text).

17. ***Sin*** is always ____________________-____________________ and never ____________________-____________________ (Daniel 8:25, More Light on the Text).

18. ***Ultimately***, all believers have the enduring, scriptural hope that evil will be ____________________ and justice will ____________________ (Daniel 8:26, More Light on the Text).

COMMITTING TO THE WORD

19. Fill in the blanks.

    "And he said, Behold, ____________________ will ____________________ thee know what shall ____________________ in the ____________________ ____________________ of the ____________________: for at the time ____________________ the end shall be" (Daniel 8:19).

WALKING IN THE WORD

20. What ***comfort*** do you derive from the fact that ***at God's appointed time***, all sin will come to an end?

    ____

    ____

    ____

    ____

"But ye shall not be so: but he that is greatest among you, let him be as the younger; and he that is chief, as he that doth serve" (Luke 22:26).

MARCH 26, 2023

THE LORD'S SUPPER

LUKE 22:14–30

Use with Bible Study Guide 4.

WORDS, PHRASES, AND DEFINITIONS

Write the following words' definitions as relates to today's lesson.

1. determined: ______________________________
2. Eucharist: ______________________________
3. Jerusalem: ______________________________
4. Judas: ______________________________
5. Passion of Christ: ______________________________
6. "Passover Lamb": ______________________________
7. remembrance: ______________________________
8. serve: ______________________________
9. "The Feast of Unleavened Bread": ______________________________
10. "the Passover": ______________________________

JUMP-STARTING THE LESSON

11. In the In Focus story, ***how did Michelle's beliefs in terms of the community*** differ from her friend Regina?

    ____

12. According to the In Focus story, we are called to be ***God's*** ______________________________ .

UNDERSTANDING THE LESSON

13. Why did the chief priests and scribes feel that ***it would not be a good time*** to set in motion their plan to kill Jesus at the Passover and Festival of Unleavened Bread (see Background)?

    ____

    ____

14. Jesus' sacrifice ***gave all of humanity*** the opportunity to be ____________________ and redeemed from the penalty of ____________________ and ____________________ (Luke 22:14–20, In Depth).

15. Jesus Christ would ***give His body as a substitute*** for ________________________ (Luke 22:14–20, In Depth).

16. "The ***suffering motif*** is consistent with Jesus' understanding of his mission as the ____________________ ____________________" (Luke 22:19–20, More Light on the Text).

17. ***True greatness*** doesn't seek self-veneration but ***is content*** with a ______________________________ ____________________ (Luke 22:26–27, More Light on the Text).

18. The ***futuristic meanings for the Passover*** are found in Jesus' prophetic words about ____________________ ____________________ (Luke 22:28–30, More Light on the Text).

COMMITTING TO THE WORD

19. Memorize and write Luke 22:19 verbatim.

____

____

____

____

____

WALKING IN THE WORD

20. What are ***you willing to do*** to make a difference in someone's life, the community, and the world?

____

____

____

____

____

____

____

____

____

____

____

"And their eyes were opened, and they knew him; and he vanished out of their sight" (Luke 24:31).

APRIL 2, 2023

THE LORD HAS RISEN INDEED!

LUKE 24:13–21, 28–35

Use with Bible Study Guide 5.

WORDS, PHRASES, AND DEFINITIONS

Write the following words' definitions as relates to today's lesson.

1. _____ burn	a. He betrayed Jesus for 30 pieces of silver.
2. _____ Cleopas	b. the first disciple that Jesus appeared to
3. _____ Emmaus	c. the meal that Jesus shared with the two men
4. _____ Jerusalem	d. the time of Jesus' trials and suffering on the Cross
5. _____ Judas	e. one of Jesus' disciples
6. _____ Lord	f. to set on fire, light
7. _____ Lord's Supper	g. the road on which two of Jesus disciples met the risen Christ
8. _____ Mary Magdalene	h. where the disciples hid after Jesus' crucifixion
9. _____ Passion Week	i. Yahweh
10. _____ Peter	j. had reported the tomb where Jesus laid was empty

JUMP-STARTING THE LESSON

11. ***What*** did Regina need to hear so that her despair over her son's heart transplant would turn to joy (see In Focus)?

____

12. ***Jesus offers*** ____________________ to us no matter the circumstances we face (see In Focus).

UNDERSTANDING THE LESSON

13. ***Peter did not believe*** the women when they reported that Jesus had risen, so he went to investigate himself (The People, Places, and Times). True False

14. Jesus ***had predicted three times*** that He would ____________________, ____________________, and be ____________________ (The People, Places, and Times).

15. Even though many of the Jews ***would not*** accept Jesus as their Messiah, what did they expect of Him (Background)?

16. ***All followers*** of Christ were under the threat of ____________________ (Luke 24:13–21, In Depth).

17. The disciples on the Emmaus Road ***immediately*** recognized Jesus on their journey (Luke 24:30, In Depth, More Light on the Text).

True False

18. In ***overcoming death***, Jesus proves to be the Lord of ____________________, the King of ____________________ (Luke 24:34, More Light on the Text).

COMMITTING TO THE WORD

19. a. Memorize and write Luke 24:33–34 verbatim. Then ***explain*** their meaning.

____

____

____

____

b. Explanations:

____

____

____

____

WALKING IN THE WORD

20. Have you ***met the risen Savior on your own Emmaus Road***? If not, why not? Share.

____

____

____

____

____

"And he said unto them, These are the words which I spake unto you, while I was yet with you, that all things must be fulfilled, which were written in the law of Moses, and in the prophets, and in the psalms, concerning me" (Luke 24:44).

APRIL 9, 2023

THE LORD APPEARS

LUKE 24:36–53

Use with Bible Study Guide 6.

WORDS, PHRASES, AND DEFINITIONS

Match the words, phrases, or names with the correct definitions.

1. _____ ascension
2. _____ Bethany
3. _____ Emmaus
4. _____ fulfilled
5. _____ Holy Spirit
6. _____ Jerusalem
7. _____ Messiah
8. _____ promise
9. _____ remission
10. _____ repentance

a. an announcement
b. The disciples were to stay in Jerusalem until they were filled with this
c. forgiveness of sin
d. Old Testament prophesies spoke of His coming
e. made complete, rendered perfect
f. Jesus went up to heaven
g. where two disciples encountered the resurrected Jesus
h. where Jesus led His disciples on the 40th day after His resurrection
i. a heartfelt sorrow for one's sins and a turning to God for help
j. the central religious and political area for Israel

JUMP-STARTING THE LESSON

11. Because of Lamar's ***past conduct***, his family was surprised when he told them that he was a ________________________ (see the In Focus story).

12. ***Jesus kept*** His ________________________ and ________________________ Old Testament prophecies (see In Focus).

UNDERSTANDING THE LESSON

13. Jesus promised that ***He would be resurrected*** on which day (Luke 24:36–43, In Depth)?

a. first   b. second   c. third   d. fourth   e. fifth

14. What ***two things*** did Jesus offer to the apostles and others to see and touch in evidence of His resurrection (Luke 24:36–43, In Depth)?

____

____

15. However, Christians ***should walk*** (believe) by ____________________ and not by ____________________ (Luke 24:36–43, In Depth).

16. Jesus reminded His disciples that ***He had previously predicted*** His ____________________, ____________________, and ____________________ (Luke 24:44–49, In Depth).

17. The ***goal*** of Jesus' death is the ____________________ of ____________________ (Luke 24:47, More Light on the Text).

18. ***Before the Resurrection***, they referred to Jesus most often as ____________________ or ____________________; ***after He appeared to Peter***, they called Him by the title of ____________________ (Luke 24:52, More Light on the Text).

COMMITTING TO THE WORD

19. Fill in the blanks.

"And said unto them, Thus it is written, and thus it behooved ____________________ to ____________________, and to ____________________ from the ____________________ the ____________________ day: And that ____________________ and ____________________ of ____________________ should be preached in his name among ____________________ ____________________, beginning at ____________________. And ye are ____________________ of these things" (Luke 24:46–48).

WALKING IN THE WORD

20. Have ***you witnessed*** for your Lord and Savior lately? Share. If not, why not?

____

____

____

____

____

____

"And they were all filled with the Holy Ghost, and began to speak with other tongues, as the Spirit gave them utterance" (Acts 2:4).

APRIL 16, 2023

THE HOLY SPIRIT COMES

ACTS 2:1–13

Use with Bible Study Guide 7.

WORDS, PHRASES, AND DEFINITIONS

Write the following words' definitions as relates to today's lesson.

1. confounded: ____________________
2. devout: ____________________
3. Holy Ghost: ____________________
4. mighty: ____________________
5. mocking: ____________________
6. Pentecost: ____________________
7. proselytes: ____________________
8. "Shavuot": ____________________
9. "transforming power": ____________________
10. wind: ____________________

JUMP-STARTING THE LESSON

11. ***Because the Holy Spirit was at work in Michelle's heart,*** what ministry did He help her to launch in her community (see In Focus story)? ____________________

____

12. ***The empowerment of the Holy Spirit, at work in one faithful heart,*** can reach out to ____________________, ____________________ ____________________ and unite a community (see In Focus).

UNDERSTANDING THE LESSON

13. ***How many days after the Jewish Passover celebration*** was Pentecost celebrated (see The People, Places, and Times)?

    a. 5 b. 10 c. 20 d. 30 e. 50

14. Many scholars believe ***which day*** marked the beginning of the Christian church (see Background)?

    ____

15. In the Upper Room, ***what two important factors*** existed on the Day of Pentecost (Acts 2:1–3, In Depth)?

    a. ______________________________

    b. ______________________________

16. ***What was the visible evidence*** of the presence of the Holy Spirit (Acts 2:1–3, In Depth, More Light on the Text)? ______________________________

17. Explain the difference between ***"being filled with the Spirit"*** and ***"the Baptism of the Spirit"*** (Acts 2:4, More Light on the Text).

    (a) ***"Being filled with the Spirit"*** is ______________________________

    (b) ***"the Baptism of the Spirit"*** is ______________________________

18. What did ***some accuse*** those whom God had filled with the Spirit of (Acts 2:13, In Depth, More Light on the Text)? ______________________________

    ____

COMMITTING TO THE WORD

19. Memorize and write Acts 2:1–4 verbatim.

    ____

    ____

    ____

WALKING IN THE WORD

20. Share a time ***when the Holy Spirit empowered you*** to come out of your comfort zone and reach out and help someone.

    ____

    ____

    ____

"For God hath not appointed us to wrath, but to obtain salvation by our Lord Jesus Christ" (1 Thessalonians 5:9).

APRIL 23, 2023

LIVING WITH HOPE

1 THESSALONIANS 4:13–5:11

Use with Bible Study Guide 8.

WORDS, PHRASES, AND DEFINITIONS

Explain the meaning.

1. "***The Day of the Lord*** will come like a thief in the night": ______

2. "The time would occur when ***people are expecting 'peace and safety'***": ______

3. "Apostle Paul described ***the unbelieving world*** as 'living in darkness'": ______

4. "Apostle Paul described ***believers*** as 'children of the light'": ______

5. "Apostle Paul instructed believers to ***put on their Christian armor*** and prepare for combat": ______

6. "The word ***'parousia'*** in Greek means 'the coming of the Lord'": ______

JUMP-STARTING THE LESSON

7. According to the In Focus story, ***when*** do thieves usually show up? ______

8. According to the In Focus story, ***how*** are believers to live until the Lord returns? ______

UNDERSTANDING THE LESSON

9. ***Who*** did Apostle Paul send to encourage the Thessalonians in their faith (see Background)?

____

10. What was ***the issue*** that apostle Paul addressed with the Thessalonians (1 Thessalonians 4:13–18, In Depth, More Light on the Text)? ______________________________

____

11. Name the ***two parts*** of the whole armor of God that apostle Paul told the believer to wear and give their functions (1 Thessalonians 5:7–11, More Light on the Text).

    a. ________________ Function: ____________________________

    b. ________________ Function: ____________________________

12. ***God's righteousness*** is worked out in ________________ and ________________ and it brings ________________ (1 Thessalonians 5:8, More Light on the Text).

13. What does the ***believer's armor*** express (1 Thessalonians 5:8, More Light on the Text)?

____

14. "Those who ***live and die in darkness and ignorance***, who sleep and are drunken in the night, instead of preparing for Christ's return, are appointed to ________________________ [God's punishment]" (1 Thessalonians 5:9, More Light on the Text).

COMMITTING TO THE WORD

15. Memorize and write 1 Thessalonians 4:16–17 verbatim.

____

____

____

____

WALKING IN THE WORD

16. How ***have you prepared*** for the "parousia"—the Lord's second coming?

____

____

____

____

> *"Now our Lord Jesus Christ himself, and God, even our Father, which hath loved us, and hath given us everlasting consolation and good hope through grace, Comfort your hearts, and stablish you in every good word and work"*
> *(2 Thessalonians 2:16–17).*

APRIL 30, 2023

HOPE COMES FROM GOD'S GRACE

2 THESSALONIANS 2:1–3, 9–17

Use with Bible Study Guide 9.

WORDS, PHRASES, AND DEFINITIONS

Match the words, phrases, or names with the correct definitions.

1. _____ antichrist	a. a defection from truth
2. _____ Deity	b. rescue, deliverance, preservation, saving
3. _____ delusion	c. consecration, purification
4. _____ "falling away"	d. the man of sin or lawlessness
5. _____ glory	e. persevere, persist in the faith
6. _____ grace	f. fraudulent, straying from orthodoxy or piety, error
7. _____ incarnation	g. the truth that Jesus was and is truly God
8. _____ salvation	h. God's favor, reward
9. _____ sanctification	i. the Son of God becoming a human being
10. _____ "stand fast"	j. honor, praise, worship, splendor, excellence to God

JUMP-STARTING THE LESSON

11. In the In Focus story, ***what conclusion*** did Warren draw about Deloris and his calling to work for the kingdom of God? ______________________________

____

____

12. What is ***God's agenda*** in terms of salvation (see In Focus)? ______________________________

____

____

____

UNDERSTANDING THE LESSON

13. List ***two things*** that apostle Paul attempted to do in this letter to the Thessalonians (see Background).

    a. ______________________________

    b. ______________________________

14. List ***two of the many warning signs*** that the Bible gives that suggest Jesus is returning soon (2 Thessalonians 2:1–3, In Depth).

    a. ______________________________

    b. ______________________________

COMMITTING TO THE WORD

15. ***The great salvation*** that believers have received (including the Thessalonians) had nothing to do with our or their own merit, but was because of God's ____________________; it was a ____________________ from God (2 Thessalonians 2:13–14, In Depth).

16. ***God had*** ____________________ and ____________________ on the Thessalonians and us and ____________________ them and us to be His ____________________ (2 Thessalonians 2:13–14, In Depth).

17. List ***four important steps*** believers should use in studying the Word of God (2 Thessalonians 2:15, More Light on the Text).

    a. ____________________ b. ____________________

    c. ____________________ d. ____________________

18. ***Apostle Paul also prayed*** that the Thessalonians might be ____________________ in the ways of God (2 Thessalonians 2:17, In Depth, More Light on the Text).

19. Fill in the blanks.

    "But we are ____________________ to give ____________________ ____________________ to ____________________ for you, brethren beloved of the Lord, because ____________________ hath from the beginning ____________________ you to ____________________ through ____________________ of the Spirit and belief of the ____________________" (2 Thessalonians 2:13).

WALKING IN THE WORD

20. Are ***good words and good works*** flowing from God's grace in your life? If not, why not?

    ____

    ____

    ____

"Blessed be the God and Father of our Lord Jesus Christ, which according to his abundant mercy hath begotten us again unto a lively hope by the resurrection of Jesus Christ from the dead" (1 Peter 1:3).

A LIVING HOPE

1 PETER 1:3–12

Use with Bible Study Guide 10.

WORDS, PHRASES, AND DEFINITIONS

Match the words, phrases, or names with the correct definitions.

1. _____ "believing faith"	a. the saints
2. _____ epistle	b. the whole person
3. _____ inheritance	c. the goal of our faith—salvation
4. _____ "lively hope"	d. a heartfelt sorrow for sin—a turning to God
5. _____ "lively stones"	e. letter
6. _____ "new birth"	f. trust in what Jesus did for believers on the Cross
7. _____ purification	g. an eternal assurance grounded in the resurrection of Christ
8. _____ repentance	h. It is dependent on the Spirit of God.
9. _____ "the prize"	i. removing the impurities from the mined substance
10. _____ "the soul"	j. something received from progenitors or predecessors

JUMP-STARTING THE LESSON

11. When Robert lost his job, ***what two things*** did he determine to do?

    a. ______________________________

    b. ______________________________

12. According to In Focus, ***a new birth*** into a living hope can be found in the ____________________ of Jesus Christ.

UNDERSTANDING THE LESSON

13. When Adam and Eve sinned against God in the Garden of Eden, ***God already*** had a plan of redemption in place (1 Peter 1:3–6, In Depth). True False

14. Through ____________________, ***we have inherited*** the promise of His kingdom here on earth (1 Peter 1:3–6, In Depth).

15. Peter encouraged the reader that although there are manifold temptations, ***we are kept*** by the ________________ of ________________ through ________________ (1 Peter 1:3–6, In Depth).

16. Name ***two purposes*** that suffering in a Christian life serves (1 Peter 1:7, More Light on the Text).

a. ____________________

b. ____________________

17. The salvation of the believer relates ***just*** to the body (1 Peter 1:9, More Light on the Text).

True False

18. ***Before Jesus' second coming,*** ________________ and ________________ are to be preached to all nations (1 Peter 1:10–11, More Light on the Text).

COMMITTING TO THE WORD

19. a. Fill in the blanks.

"That the ________________ of your ________________, being much more ________________ than of ________________ that perisheth, though it be ________________ with ________________, might be found unto ________________ and ________________ and ________________ at the appearing of ________________ ________________" (1 Peter 1:7).

b. Explanation:

____

____

____

WALKING IN THE WORD

20. ***List ways*** that you can have an impact of hope on your family or community.

____

____

____

____

"According as his divine power hath given unto us all things that pertain unto life and godliness, through the knowledge of him that hath called us to glory and virtue" (2 Peter 1:3).

MAY 14, 2023

EQUIPPED WITH HOPE

2 PETER 1:4–14

Use with Bible Study Guide 11.

WORDS, PHRASES, AND DEFINITIONS

Write the following words' definitions as relates to today's lesson.

1. brotherly kindness: ______________________________
2. charity: ______________________________
3. corruption: ______________________________
4. faith: ______________________________
5. godliness: ______________________________
6. knowledge: ______________________________
7. patience: ______________________________
8. temperance: ______________________________
9. "the truth": ______________________________
10. virtue: ______________________________

JUMP-STARTING THE LESSON

11. According to In Focus, faith ***is equivalent*** to blind optimism.

    True False

12. Believers ***must take full advantage*** of the godly resources available to each of us (see In Focus).

    True False

UNDERSTANDING THE LESSON

13. ***After Pentecost***, many believers were ____________, ____________, ____________, and ____________ (see The People, Places, and Times).

14. How did ***Stephen***, one of the first deacons, die (see The People, Places, and Times)?

____

____

15. How did ***apostle James***, the brother of John, die (see The People, Places, and Times)?

____

____

16. What was the ***two-fold purpose*** of Peter writing 2 Peter (see Background)?

a. ____

b. ____

17. A believer's spiritual growth is an ***ongoing process***, during which there is constant ____________________, ____________________, and ____________________ (2 Peter 1:5–9, In Depth).

18. By reminding believers of ***God's divine*** ____________________, ____________________, and ____________________, Peter was reminding them to never forget the basis for their ____________________ (2 Peter 1:12, More Light on the Text).

COMMITTING TO THE WORD

19. Fill in the blanks.

"And beside this, giving all diligence, add to your faith ____________________; and to ____________________; And to ____________________; and to ____________________; and to ____________________; And to ____________________; and to ____________________" (2 Peter 1:5–7).

WALKING IN THE WORD

20. ***Reread 2 Peter 1:1–7 and identify*** below which of the godly characteristics are currently active in your life and which traits you need "to make every effort to add to your faith."

____

____

____

____

____

____

____

"As every man hath received the gift, even so minister the same one to another, as good stewards of the manifold grace of God" (1 Peter 4:10).

MAY 21, 2023

HOPE THROUGH STEWARDSHIP

1 PETER 4:1–11

Use with Bible Study Guide 12.

WORDS, PHRASES, AND DEFINITIONS

Write the following words' definitions as relates to today's lesson.

1. body: ______
2. debauchery: ______
3. "God's grace": ______
4. holiness: ______
5. lasciviousness: ______
6. love: ______
7. "Pente": ______
8. sanctification: ______
9. sober: ______
10. "the kingdom of God": ______

JUMP-STARTING THE LESSON

11. According to the In Focus story, ***why*** was Michelle filled with joy? ______

______

______

12. ***The clarion call of Acts 1:8*** expresses that after the Holy Ghost is come upon you, you will be witnesses where (see In Focus)?

a. ______ b. ______

c. ______ d. ______

UNDERSTANDING THE LESSON

13. ***Why*** were the disciples gathered in the Upper Room (see The People, Places, and Times)?

____

14. What were ***three requirements*** to be a replacement of Judas (the disciple that betrayed Jesus for 30 pieces of silver) [see The People, Places, and Times]?

a. ____

b. ____

c. ____

15. What must followers of Christ ***put on*** in order ***not to*** fulfill the lusts of the flesh (1 Peter 4:1–2, In Depth)?

____

16. In preparation for the end times, ***what three things*** did apostle Peter admonish the faithful to do (1 Peter 4:7–9)?

a. ______________ b. ______________ c. ______________

17. As believers, ***what covered our sins*** (1 Peter 4:8, More Light on the Text)? ______________

____

18. What ***two kinds of gifts*** did apostle Peter speak of in today's text (1 Peter 4:11, More Light on the Text)?

a. ____

b. ____

COMMITTING TO THE WORD

19. Fill in the blanks.

"Forasmuch then as ______________ hath ______________ for us in the ______________,

______________ yourselves likewise with the ______________: for he that hath

______________ in the ______________ hath ______________ from ______________;

That he no longer should live the rest of his time in the ______________ to the ______________

of men, but to the ______________ of ______________" (1 Peter 4:1–2).

WALKING IN THE WORD

20. Share ways that ***you have overcome habits of the flesh*** to walk in the newness of life.

____

____

____

"The Lord is not slack concerning his promise, as some men count slackness; but is longsuffering to us-ward, not willing that any should perish, but that all should come to repentance" (2 Peter 3:9).

MAY 28, 2023

HOPE IN THE DAY OF THE LORD

2 PETER 3:1–15A

Use with Bible Study Guide 13.

WORDS, PHRASES, AND DEFINITIONS

Match the words, phrases, or names with the correct definitions.

1. _____ apostle	a. mockers; false teachers who mark the truth
2. _____ coming	b. Jesus' second coming
3. _____ epistle	c. arouse completely
4. _____ lusts	d. pertaining to being sincere, without hidden motives or pretense
5. _____ parousia	e. messenger, envoy
6. _____ perdition	f. strong desires for something forbidden
7. _____ pure	g. appearing
8. _____ scoffers	h. impious, destitute of reverential awe toward God
9. _____ "stir up"	i. destruction, annihilation, ruin
10. _____ ungodly	j. a letter, correspondence

JUMP-STARTING THE LESSON

11. According to In Focus, what is ***a promise***? ____________________

____

12. ***Who*** is the one that keeps every one of His promises (see In Focus)? ____________________

UNDERSTANDING THE LESSON

13. ***Give two reasons why*** apostle Peter wrote 2 Peter (see Background).

a. ____________________

b. ____________________

14. What is the time period for ***"the last days"*** (2 Peter 3:1–4, In Depth)? ______________________________

____

____

15. The scoffers do not believe ***the truth*** of ______________________ ______________________ (2 Peter 3:5–9, In Depth).

16. Apostle Peter believed that the reason ***Jesus has not yet returned*** is because God is ______________________ (2 Peter 3:9, More Light on the Text).

17. ***List three things*** that apostle Peter described as a part of an unprecedented devastation that will happen on the Day of the Lord (2 Peter 3:10, More Light on the Text).

 a. ____

 b. ____

 c. ____

18. ***List three reasons why*** the new heaven and new earth (promised in Isaiah 65:17) ***will be perfect*** (2 Peter 3:13, More Light on the Text).

 a. ____

 b. ____

 c. ____

COMMITTING TO THE WORD

19. Memorize and write 2 Peter 3:8–9 verbatim.

____

____

____

____

WALKING IN THE WORD

20. Until Jesus returns, ***what are you doing*** to help build His kingdom?

____

____

____

____

____

"And one cried unto another, and said, Holy, holy, holy, is the LORD of hosts: the whole earth is full of his glory" (Isaiah 6:3).

JUNE 4, 2023

HOLY, HOLY, HOLY

ISAIAH 6:1–8

Use with Bible Study Guide 1.

WORDS, PHRASES, AND DEFINITIONS

Write the following words' definitions as relates to today's lesson.

1. death: ______________________________
2. glory: ______________________________
3. holy: ______________________________
4. iniquity: ______________________________
5. Isaiah: ______________________________
6. King Uzziah: ______________________________
7. "train":______________________________
8. "the seraphim": ______________________________
9. undone: ______________________________
10. woe: ______________________________

JUMP-STARTING THE LESSON

11. What did Warren and Deloris do in the midst of praying for Warren's company (see the In Focus story)?

____

____

____

12. According to In Focus, who did Warren acknowledge to his boss for giving him insight into how to solve the company's problem?

____

____

UNDERSTANDING THE LESSON

13. Name ***four Major Prophets*** that prophesied in 8th-century B.C. in the northern and southern kingdoms of Israel and Judah (see Background).

    a. ______________________ b. ______________________

    c. ______________________ d. ______________________

14. True *worship* ***recognizes*** God's ______________________ (Isaiah 6:1–4, In Depth).

15. True *worship* ***acknowledges*** ______________________ (Isaiah 6:5, In Depth).

16. True *worship* ***receives*** God's ______________________ (Isaiah 6:6–7, In Depth).

17. True *worship* ***responds*** to God's ______________________ (Isaiah 6:8, In Depth).

18. Isaiah understood that he was committing to represent God's ______________________ ______________________ and ______________________ on earth (Isaiah 6:8, More Light on the Text).

COMMITTING TO THE WORD

19. Write Isaiah 6:5 verbatim from memory.

WALKING IN THE WORD

20. Have you had a proper vision of the ***majesty of God*** and His holiness so that you have come to understand just how ***sinful and unworthy we all are***? If so, share; if not, write a prayer praying for such a vision.

"And in that day shall ye say, Praise the LORD, call upon his name, declare his doings among the people, make mention that his name is exalted" (Isaiah 12:4).

JUNE 11, 2023

GIVE THANKS

ISAIAH 12

Use with Bible Study Guide 2.

WORDS, PHRASES, AND DEFINITIONS

Match the words, phrases, or names with the correct definitions.

1. _____ comfort	a. to be saved from the guilt and punishment of sin
2. _____ El Yeshuah	b. to speak out, confess, sing, and give thanks
3. _____ excellence	c. in Hebrew it means "to exult God with music"
4. _____ millennium	d. a servant of the Lord called to encourage God's faithful people
5. _____ name	e. have pity, compassion, and consolation
6. _____ praise	f. a name given to Jesus Christ by the Angel Gabriel
7. _____ prophet	g. it communicates the character or reputation of a person
8. _____ salvation	h. the great reign of Christ on earth
9. _____ sing	i. majesty, power, splendor
10. _____ *tehillah*	j. to be a part of continued praise with music

JUMP-STARTING THE LESSON

11. What was Monique's favorite part of her family's Juneteenth gathering (see In Focus story)? ____________

____

12. Festivals and celebrations are a great way to acknowledge and express ____________ to ____________ for His many wonderful ____________ (see In Focus story).

UNDERSTANDING THE LESSON

13. Name two prophets who were blessed with a vision of the reign of Christ on earth (see Background).

a. ____________ b. ____________

14. In the future reign of Christ, what two things will God's people praise Him for (Isaiah 12:1–3, In Depth)?

a. ______________________________

b. ______________________________

15. What did Isaiah praise God for a thousand years before its still-future fulfillment (Isaiah 12:1–3, In Depth)?

____

____

16. Trust implies what three things?

a. ______________________________

b. ______________________________ and

c. ______________________________ (Isaiah 12:1–3, In Depth)?

17. What did Isaiah instruct those who belong to God to do (Isaiah 12:4, More Light on the Text)?

____

____

____

18. Why did Isaiah instruct the inhabitant of Zion to cry out and shout (Isaiah 12:6, More Light on the Text)?

____

____

____

COMMITTING TO THE WORD

19. Write Isaiah 12:2 verbatim from memory.

____

____

____

WALKING IN THE WORD

20. Write your own ***prayer, poem, or song lifting up the name of Jesus***.

____

____

____

____

"Wherefore the Lord said, Forasmuch as this people draw near me with their mouth, and with their lips do honour me, but have removed their heart far from me, and their fear toward me is taught by the precept of men" (Isaiah 29:13).

JUNE 18, 2023

MEANINGLESS WORSHIP

ISAIAH 29:9–16A

Use with Bible Study Guide 3.

WORDS, PHRASES, AND DEFINITIONS

Write the following words' definitions as relates to today's lesson.

1. blindness: ______________________________
2. counsel: ______________________________
3. heart: ______________________________
4. mouth: ______________________________
5. omnipotent: ______________________________
6. omnipresent: ______________________________
7. omniscient: ______________________________
8. "stay yourself": ______________________________
9. "stumbling block": ______________________________
10. vision: ______________________________

JUMP-STARTING THE LESSON

11. According to the In Focus, we can get so caught up in the ***daily burdens and blessings of life*** that we forget the ______________ ______________.
12. God must be worshiped in ______________ and in ______________ (see In Focus).

UNDERSTANDING THE LESSON

13. God told Isaiah that his ministry would be ______________ (see Background)?
14. During Isaiah's ministry, many of Judea's citizens were drunk on the cup of ______________ ______________ (Isaiah 29:9–12, In Depth).

15. The ***Judeans claimed to be children of God***, but they lived their lives in ____________________ (Isaiah 29:13–14, In Depth).

16. The people (Judeans) tried to veil their ***hypocritical religious practices*** from the One who is ____________________ (knows all), ____________________ (is present everywhere), and ____________________ (all powerful) (Isaiah 29:15, More Light on the Text).

17. God would ____________________ Israel in the same manner the potter ____________________ the vessel on the wheel (Isaiah 29:16a, More Light on the Text).

18. Today, we must constantly be reminded that ***meaningless worship*** is an ____________________ to God (Isaiah 29:16a, More Light on the Text).

COMMITTING TO THE WORD

19. Fill in the blanks.

"Wherefore the Lord said, Forasmuch as this people ____________________ ____________________ ____________________ with their ____________________, and with their ____________________ do ____________________ me, but have ____________________ their ____________________ far from me, and their fear toward me is taught by the ____________________ of men:" (Isaiah 29:13.)

WALKING IN THE WORD

20. What have you done when you saw your worship was becoming routine or meaningless?

____

____

____

____

____

____

____

____

____

____

____

"For, behold, I create new heavens and a new earth: and the former shall not be remembered, nor come into mind. But be ye glad and rejoice for ever in that which I create: for, behold, I create Jerusalem a rejoicing, and her people a joy" (Isaiah 65:17–18).

JUNE 25, 2023

THE GLORIOUS NEW CREATION

ISAIAH 65:17–21, 23–25

Use with Bible Study Guide 4.

WORDS, PHRASES, AND DEFINITIONS

Write the following words' definitions as relates to today's lesson.

1. cosmologists: ____________________
2. create: ____________________
3. earth: ____________________
4. glad: ____________________
5. heavens: ____________________
6. "Jerusalem's Prophetic Destiny": ____________________
7. "Milky Way": ____________________
8. rejoice: ____________________
9. theologians: ____________________
10. trouble: ____________________

JUMP-STARTING THE LESSON

11. According to In Focus, scholars and cosmologists both agree that the universe is ____________________ ____________________.

12. According to In Focus, at the end of time God will create a new ____________________ and ____________________ that will extend into all ____________________.

UNDERSTANDING THE LESSON

13. Isaiah sees a ____________________ and ____________________ ____________________ future for the nation of Israel (see Background).

14. Name four attributes of the new heavens and earth (Isaiah 65:19, More Light on the Text).

a. ______________________ b. ______________________

c. ______________________ d. ______________________

15. The new millennium will bring forth from God ______________________ (Isaiah 65:20, More Light on the Text).

16. When man rebelled against God and fell into sin, all of creation ______________________ (Isaiah 65:17–21, In Depth).

17. Name two things that happened when Adam and Eve sinned (Isaiah 65:23–25, In Depth).

a. ______________________

b. ______________________

18. In the new heaven and earth, there will be no more ______________________ and ______________________ (Isaiah 65:25, More Light on the Text).

COMMITTING TO THE WORD

19. Write Isaiah 65:17–18 verbatim from memory.

____

____

____

____

____

WALKING IN THE WORD

20. Will you be a part of God's glorious new creation?

Yes _____ No _____

Explain.

____

____

____

____

____

"They kept also the feast of tabernacles, as it is written, and offered the daily burnt offerings by number, according to the custom, as the duty of every day required" (Ezra 3:4).

JULY 2, 2023

JOYFUL WORSHIP RESTORED

EZRA 3:1–7

Use with Bible Study Guide 5.

WORDS, PHRASES, AND DEFINITIONS

Match the words, phrases, or names with the correct definitions.

1. _____ altar
2. _____ Feast of Booths
3. _____ "freewill offerings"
4. _____ "gather together"
5. _____ Jeshua
6. _____ Josiah
7. _____ Lebanon
8. _____ Moses
9. _____ tabernacles
10. _____ Zerubbabel

a. tent sanctuaries used by Israelites during the Exodus
b. the high priest at the time Judah went into Babylonian exile
c. God gave the law to him
d. the appointed governor of Judah
e. showed cohesiveness and unity among the people of Israel
f. used as the focus for a religious ritual
g. signifies that one is incited or impelled to give voluntarily
h. a harvest festival that lasts for one week
i. a king who sought to cleanse and restore true worship
j. the cedar trees to build the temple came from this place

JUMP-STARTING THE LESSON

11. Why did Andre stop going to church and praising and worshiping God (see In Focus)?

____

12. Believers should ask God to help us maintain ____________________ ____________________ of ***God who is worthy to be praised*** (see In Focus).

UNDERSTANDING THE LESSON

13. What led to the ***urgent construction of the Lord's altar*** by the Israelites (Ezra 3:3, More Light on the Text)?

____

14. The Feast of Tabernacles is similar to our ______________________ and commemorates the ______________________ years the Israelites worshiped in ______________________ in the ______________________ (Ezra 3:1–5, In Depth).

15. Who preserved the pieces that belonged in the Temple and returned them when the children of Israel returned to Jerusalem (Ezra 3:6–7, In Depth)? ______________________

____

____

16. The true Temple was the renewed ______________________ among the people (Ezra 3:6–7, In Depth).

17. Which offering served as the primary sacrificial ceremony in reverence to the Lord among the people of Israel (Ezra 3:6–7, More Light on the Text)? ______________________

____

____

18. Only Israelites helped to reconstruct the temple (Ezra 3:6–7, More Light on the Text).

True False

COMMITTING TO THE WORD

19. Write Ezra 3:5 verbatim from memory.

____

____

____

20. Explain the meaning of the verse above.

____

____

____

WALKING IN THE WORD

21. Have you done anything special to enhance your own ***worship experience*** to make it more meaningful? Why? Why not?

____

____

____

"And they sang together by course in praising and giving thanks unto the LORD; because he is good, for his mercy endureth for ever toward Israel. And all the people shouted with a great shout, when they praised the LORD, because the foundation of the house of the LORD was laid" (Ezra 3:11).

JULY 9, 2023

TEMPLE RESTORED

EZRA 3:8–13

Use with Bible Study Guide 6.

WORDS, PHRASES, AND DEFINITIONS

Match the words, phrases, or names with the correct definitions.

1. _____ "ancient men"
2. _____ disenfranchised
3. _____ house
4. _____ Jeshua
5. _____ joy
6. _____ King David
7. _____ King Cyrus
8. _____ Levites
9. _____ remnant
10. _____ Zerubbabel

a. mansion, palace, or dwelling place
b. They served as assistants to the priests in the worship system.
c. a worshipper who knew how to get God's attention with music
d. the remainder, the residue or survivors
e. tribal fathers (elders)
f. expressed in praises
g. the Jewish governor
h. He was Israel's high priest.
i. He permitted the Jews to return to Jerusalem and rebuild their temple.
j. the marginalized

JUMP-STARTING THE LESSON

11. According to the In Focus story, after Vice President Harris was inaugurated, Betty shouted for ____________________ and gave ____________________ to God for His goodness.

12. God's word promises that he would cause us to ____________________ in ____________________ ____________________ and bring us to a place of ____________________ (see In Focus story).

UNDERSTANDING THE LESSON

13. How long were the Israelites ***in exile in Babylon as prophesied*** by Jeremiah (see Background)?

a. 10 years   b. 30 years   c. 40 years   d. 50 years   e. 60 years   f. 70 years

14. In regard to rebuilding the Temple, what three things were the ***people called upon*** to do by their leaders (see Background)?

a. ______________________________

b. ______________________________

c. ______________________________

15. In a broader sense, what did ***rebuilding the Temple*** mean in relation to the Israelites ***relationship with God*** (Ezra 3:8–9, In Depth)? ______________________________

____

16. Why did the tribal fathers have mixed emotions about the new Temple (Ezra 3:12–13, In Depth)?

____

____

17. Their deliverance from captivity in Babylon brought shouts of great joy from the tribal fathers (Ezra 3:12–13).

True False

18. The wailing and rejoicing from the tribal fathers could not be discerned (Ezra 3:12–13).

True False

COMMITTING TO THE WORD

19. Fill in the blanks.

"And they ______________ ______________ by course in ______________ and ______________ unto the ______________; because he is ______________, for his ______________ endureth ______________ toward Israel. And all the people ______________ with a great ______________, when they ______________ the LORD, because the ______________ of the house of the LORD was ______________" (Ezra 3:11).

WALKING IN THE WORD

20. Reflect on a time in your life ***when you have seen God move*** on your behalf to restore you after a moment of defeat or failure. Share.

____

____

____

"And the children of Israel, the priests, and the Levites, and the rest of the children of the captivity, kept the dedication of this house of God with joy" (Ezra 6:16).

JULY 16, 2023

DEDICATION OF THE TEMPLE

EZRA 6:13–22

Use with Bible Study Guide 7.

WORDS, PHRASES, AND DEFINITIONS

Write the following words' definitions as relates to today's lesson.

1. archetype: ______
2. "consecrate themselves": ______
3. dedication: ______
4. Feast of Unleavened Bread: ______
5. King Darius: ______
6. Passover: ______
7. prophesying: ______
8. purified: ______
9. "sin offering": ______
10. "The perfect sacrifice": ______

JUMP-STARTING THE LESSON

11. What did Anthony and Angie make sure that they had in their new house (see In Focus story)?

______

______

______

______

12. The children of Israel celebrated the ***successful rebuilding and dedication of God's Temple*** just in time for ______ (see In Focus).

UNDERSTANDING THE LESSON

13. Who decreed and gave clearance that the children of Israel rebuild the temple (see Background)?

____

____

14. Who were to bare the expenses of rebuilding the temple (see Background)?

____

____

15. List one reason why the Israelites rejoiced over the rebuilding of the Temple (Ezra 6:13–16, In Depth)?

____

16. The house or Temple they built belonged to ____________________ (Ezra 6:13–16, In Depth).

17. List at least three things that the sin offering at the dedication consisted of (Ezra 6:18, More Light on the Text). a. ____________________ b. ____________________ c. ____________________

18. What did the fact that "the Levites were purified together" mean (Ezra 6:20, More Light on the Text)?

____

____

COMMITTING TO THE WORD

19. Write Ezra 6:16 verbatim from memory.

____

____

____

WALKING IN THE WORD

20. ***Boast in the Lord*** below with great joy, giving Him glory for everything He has done in your life.

____

____

____

____

____

____

"So we fasted and besought our God for this: and he was intreated of us" (Ezra 8:23).

JULY 23, 2023

FASTING AND PRAYING

EZRA 8:21–23

Use with Bible Study Guide 8.

STATEMENTS

Explain the meaning.

1. "Ezra moved from a ***prophetic role to a leadership role***": ______________________________

____

2. "Ezra realized if they were to have safe passage, it would only happen with the help of God": ___________

____

____

3. "As a result of the fast, ***the Lord heard their prayer and supplications*** and showed Ezra the plan for a safe journey": ______________________________

____

4. "Their path may not have been in a straight line or the most obvious way, but it was the way the Lord had ordained": ______________________________

____

5. "It is important to ***pray when you fast***": ______________________________

____

6. "Ezra, the priest of Yahweh": ______________________________

____

JUMP-STARTING THE LESSON

7. According to the In Focus story, what did Monique do when she found that her job took her into some unsavory neighborhoods? ______________________________

____

8. According to In Focus, ____________________ and ____________________ move God to action in ____________________ situations.

UNDERSTANDING THE LESSON

9. Ezra was a ____________________, well versed in the ____________________ ____________________ (see The People, Places, and Times).
10. The Persian king had been convinced of ____________________ protection for the returning ____________________ (see Background).
11. The caravan was made up of ____________________ men, women, and children and they traveled over ____________________ miles (Ezra 8:23, In Depth).
12. Explain the phrase, "So we fasted and besought our God for this, and he was intreated of us" (Ezra 8:23, More Light on the Text). ____
____
13. God desires the ____________________ and ____________________ of humans submitted in ____________________ and ____________________ ____________________ on His loving protection and will toward them (Ezra 8:23, More Light on the Text).
14. God ____________________ and ____________________ those who seek Him with a ____________________ ____________________ and ____________________ (Ezra 8:23, More Light on the Text).

COMMITTING TO THE WORD

15. Write Ezra 8:21 verbatim from memory.

____
____
____

WALKING IN THE WORD

16. Share a time when you fasted and prayed over dire circumstances.

____
____
____

"And I said unto them, Ye are holy unto the Lord; the vessels are holy also; and the silver and the gold are a freewill offering unto the Lord God of your fathers" (Ezra 8:28).

JULY 30, 2023

GIFTS FOR THE TEMPLE

EZRA 8:24–30

Use with Bible Study Guide 9.

WORDS, PHRASES, AND DEFINITIONS

Match the words, phrases, or names with the correct definitions.

1. _____ consecrated	a. a mediator between God and humanity
2. _____ Ezra	b. God's blessings are appropriated through this
3. _____ God's instrument	c. Jerusalem
4. _____ house of God	d. one of 12 priests who accompanied Ezra and the caravan
5. _____ ordination	e. bowls
6. _____ prayer	f. a priest who returned from the exile with Zerubbabel
7. _____ priest	g. to be set apart for the sole purpose of service to God
8. _____ Sherebiah	h. set apart as holy unto God
9. _____ "twenty basons"	i. a vessel God can use in His service
10. _____ Zion	j. the temple, the church, your body

JUMP-STARTING THE LESSON

11. In the In Focus story, what were the author's feelings on the time he was homeless?

____

____

____

12. How did the author show his thankfulness (see In Focus)? _______________________

____

____

____

UNDERSTANDING THE LESSON

13. List seven areas that made up Israel (see The People, Places, and Times).

a. ______________________ b. ______________________

c. ______________________ d. ______________________

e. ______________________ f. ______________________

g. ______________________

14. How may years had passed between the dedication of the temple in 516 B.C. ad the arrival of Ezra in Jerusalem (see Background)?

a. 10 b. 25 c. 35 d. 48 e. 50 f. 58

COMMITTING TO THE WORD

15. Ezra declared the money that they were traveling with as what (Background)? ______________________

____

____

16. Ezra, the priest, led a second group of exiles back to Judah and Jerusalem approximately how many years after the first group had returned (Ezra 8:24–27, In Depth)?

a. 20 b. 40 c. 60 d. 80 e. 100 f. 110

17. The vessels are ______________________ also (Ezra 8:28, More Light on the Text).

18. The rebuilt temple was blessed with the people's ______________________ ______________________ (Ezra 8:29, More Light on the Text).

19. Fill in the blanks.

"And I said unto them, ______________________ are ______________________ unto the ______________________; the ______________________ are ______________________ also; and the ______________________ and the ______________________ are a ______________________ offering unto the Lord God of your fathers" (Ezra 8:28).

WALKING IN THE WORD

20. Have you dedicated your possessions unto the Lord? Why? Why not?

____

____

____

"And all the congregation of them that were come again out of the captivity made booths, and sat under the booths: for since the days of Jeshua the son of Nun unto that day had not the children of Israel done so. And there was very great gladness" (Nehemiah 8:17).

FESTIVAL OF BOOTHS

NEHEMIAH 8:13–18

Use with Bible Study Guide 10.

WORDS, PHRASES, AND DEFINITIONS

Match the words, phrases, or names with the correct definitions.

1. _____ Juneteeth	a. celebration with holy convocation and joyfulness
2. _____ Levites	b. bondage
3. _____ Jerusalem	c. a gathering of people in one place
4. _____ *Sukkot*	d. first five books of the Bible containing Mosaic Law
5. _____ booths	e. ram's horn blown as an alarm
6. _____ captivity	f. celebration commemorating African-American freedom
7. _____ assembly	g. language of business for Babylon and later Persia
8. _____ Pentateuch	h. center of national worship
9. _____ shofar	i. temporary shelters
10. _____ Aramaic	j. chosen by God to serve in the Temple

JUMP-STARTING THE LESSON

11. How was news of the Feast of the Booths spread (see More Light on the Text)?

a. ______________________________

b. ______________________________

12. What is ***another name for the Festival of Booths*** (see In Depth)? ______________

UNDERSTANDING THE LESSON

13. The ***participation in the Festival of Booths*** was lower than it had been with other celebration since the days of Joshua (More Light on the Text). True False

14. What was read to the people during this celebration of the Festival of Booths, and ***how long did the celebration last*** (More Light on the Text)?

a. ____________________

b. ____________________

15. On which day did the ***"solemn assembly"*** take place (Focal Verses)? ____________________

16. What were the ***booths*** to be made of (In Depth)? ____________________

____

____

17. What made the Festival of Booths such ***a joyous occasion*** (In Depth)? ____________________

____

____

____

18. ***What happened*** to the Children of Israel each day that the book of the Law was read (In Depth)? ____________________

____

____

____

COMMITTING TO THE WORD

19. Fill in the blanks.

"And all the ____________ of them that were come again out of the ____________ made booths, and sat under the booths: for since the days of ____________ the son of ____________ unto that day had not the ____________ ____________ done so. And there was very great ____________" (Nehemiah 8:17).

WALKING IN THE WORD

20. List ways that you can ***incorporate God*** into every aspect of your next joyous occasion.

____

____

____

____

"And the seed of Israel separated themselves from all strangers, and stood and confessed their sins, and the iniquities of their fathers" (Nehemiah 9:2).

AUGUST 13, 2023

COMMUNITY OF CONFESSION

NEHEMIAH 9:2, 6–7, 9–10, 30–36

Use with Bible Study Guide 11.

WORDS, PHRASES, AND DEFINITIONS

Match the words, phrases, or names with the correct definitions.

1. _____ prayer	a. the vehicle toward our freedom from sin
2. _____ Shechaniah	b. the worship of other gods
3. _____ repent	c. holiday commemorating Israel's escape from slavery
4. _____ disobedience	d. the son of Jehiel
5. _____ confession	e. to seek forgiveness and turn away from transgressions
6. _____ faith	f. petition, complaint, praise, thanksgiving, and confession
7. _____ idolatry	g. not doing what is ordered or commanded
8. _____ Passover	h. awe-inspiring and holy, not cruel or capricious
9. _____ Mount Gerizim	i. represents the blessing of God for obedience
10. _____ "terrible"	j. without this, it's impossible to please God

JUMP-STARTING THE LESSON

11. What is the beginning of a person's ***journey of faith*** (see Discuss the Meaning)?

    a. ______________________________

    b. ______________________________

12. What does ***confession of sins*** include (see Discuss the Meaning)? ______________________________

UNDERSTANDING THE LESSON

13. "The ***seed of Israel*** separated themselves from all strangers" because it fell into idolatrous practices through marrying people from other nations (More Light on the Text). True False

14. "And ____________________ the son of ____________________, one of the sons of Elam, answered and said unto ____________________, We have ____________________ against our ____________________, and have taken ____________________ ____________________ the people of the land: yet now there is in ____________________ concerning this thing." (Ezra 10:2, Background)

15. The Word of God can do what four things (In Depth)? ____________________

16. In what chapter is the longest prayer in the Bible found (More Light on the Text)? ____________________

17. Why did the people of Israel confess not only their own sins but also "the iniquities of their fathers" (More Light on the Text)? ____________________

18. What does Mount Ebal represent (More Light on the Text)? ____________________

COMMITTING TO THE WORD

19. Write Nehemiah 9:2 verbatim from memory.

20. Write an explanation for the Scripture above.

"Also that day they offered great sacrifices, and rejoiced: for God had made them rejoice with great joy: the wives also and the children rejoiced: so that the joy of Jerusalem was heard even afar off" (Nehemiah 12:43).

AUGUST 20, 2023

DEDICATION OF THE WALL

NEHEMIAH 12:27–36, 38, 43

Use with Bible Study Guide 12.

WORDS, PHRASES, AND DEFINITIONS

Match the words, phrases, or names with the correct definitions.

1. _____ purified
2. _____ Artaxerxes
3. _____ restoration
4. _____ Nehemiah
5. _____ remnant
6. _____ Levites
7. _____ *kohen*
8. _____ rejoiced
9. _____ purification
10. _____ dedication

a. gladdened
b. those left behind
c. cleansed and made undefiled ceremonially
d. a religious ceremony in which a person or a thing is set aside or consecrated to God's service
e. symbolized the washing away of their previous trespasses and gross misconduct and their renewed clean and righteous relationship with God
f. the word "priests" in Hebrew
g. the priests—the descendants of Levi, specially set aside by God for His service
h. returning something to its previous condition
i. granted permission to the Jews to rebuild the walls of Jerusalem
j. book that occurs during the post-exilic history of the Children of Israel

JUMP-STARTING THE LESSON

11. What two things did God restore by ***allowing the wall to be rebuilt*** (In Depth)?

a. ____

b. ____

12. What had ***God promised to the children of Israel*** after they returned from exile (People, Places and Times)?

____

____

UNDERSTANDING THE LESSON

13. ***God*** always ***calls extraordinary people*** to do His will (More Light on the Text). True False

14. "Remember, I ____________ thee, the word that thou ____________ thy servant ____________, saying, If ye transgress, I will ____________ you abroad among the nations: But if ye turn unto me, and keep my ____________, and do them; though there were of you ____________ ____________ unto the uttermost part of the ____________, yet will I ____________ them from thence, and will bring them unto the place that I have ____________ to set my name there" (Nehemiah 1:8–9).

15. ***Why did God remove the children of Israel*** from their land and take everything from them (People, Places and Times)? ____________

16. In addition to singing, how else did the children of Israel ***celebrate the joyous occasion*** (Focal Verses)?

17. Name as many people as you can who took part in the ceremony. (Nehemiah 12:32–36)

COMMITTING TO THE WORD

18. Write Nehemiah 12:43 verbatim from memory.

19. Explain what was happening in the Scripture above.

"And I commanded the Levites that they should cleanse themselves, and that they should come and keep the gates, to sanctify the sabbath day. Remember me, O my God, concerning this also, and spare me according to the greatness of thy mercy" (Nehemiah 13:22).

AUGUST 27, 2023

SABBATH REFORMS

NEHEMIAH 13:15–22

Use with Bible Study Guide 13.

WORDS, PHRASES, AND DEFINITIONS

Match the words, phrases, or names with the correct definitions.

1. _____ Sabbath	a. "strove physically, confronted, made a complaint"
2. _____ testified	b. "to defile, pollute, or desecrate"
3. _____ Ten Commandments	c. a day to set aside for worship and praise to God
4. _____ ceremonial law	d. bore witness, affirmed solemnly
5. _____ sanctify	e. found in Exodus 31:14
6. _____ "contended"	f. "bad, disagreeable, malignant, displeasing"
7. _____ The Lord's Day	g. day of cleansing from work; time to rest
8. _____ civil law	h. separation from ordinary use to a sacred purpose
9. _____ "profane"	i. located in Leviticus 23:3
10. _____ "evil"	j. moral law

JUMP-STARTING THE LESSON

11. ***What*** things did Nehemiah refuse to allow to occur on the Sabbath (More Light on the Text)?

a. ____

b. ____

c. ____

12. ***What did God require*** of the Israelites when He first established the nation (People, Places and Times)?

____

____

____

UNDERSTANDING THE LESSON

13. God only provided the children of Israel with part of what they needed so they would learn to trust Him more (People, Places and Times). True False

14. Other than the wall, ***what three things*** did the Israelites have to restore (Background)? ____________

____

____

15. ***What*** document ***evolved*** from the reading of the law (Background)? ____________

____

16. What was a ***sign*** from the Israelites ***that God truly ruled Israel*** (In Depth)? ____________

____

17. What did it mean ***to disobey the Sabbath*** (In Depth)? ____________

____

18. How did Nehemiah challenge the leaders of Judah in their ***conduct regarding the Sabbath*** (In Depth)?

____

____

COMMITTING TO THE WORD

19. Fill in the blanks.

"And I ____________ the Levites that they should ____________ themselves, and that they should come and keep the gates, to ____________ the sabbath day. ____________ ____________, O my God, concerning this also, and ____________ ____________ according to the ____________ of thy ____________" (Nehemiah 13:22).

WALKING IN THE WORD

20. List ways in which you will try to ***honor the Sabbath and keep it holy.***

____

____

____

____

____

ANSWER KEY

SEPTEMBER-NOVEMBER 2022

ANSWER KEY TO LESSON 1

1. adversaries: believers who reject Christ and disobey God
2. apostasy: a rejection of the sacrifice of Christ; a rejection of His salvation
3. "a true heart": genuine, sincere, and faithful
4. common: unhallowed
5. "God's adversaries": the enemies of God
6. "hold fast": hold on to
7. insult: reduce the honor that is due to another person
8. provoke: irritate or exasperate
9. "the blood of the covenant": an expression used of the blood that established the Old Covenant and also of the blood of Jesus that established the New Covenant
10. "The day": a day in which God will judge
11. Angie had not forgiven herself for her sins.
12. faith, Christ, forgiven, new life
13. The "Holy of Holies" was located in the innermost sanctuary of the Temple.
14. Jesus Christ, faith
15. On "the Day of Atonement," the High Priest made reconciling sacrifices for the sins of the entire nation.
16. faith
17. We should approach the throne of grace through (a) the mediation of Christ and (b) through Christ's sacrificial death.
18. An "apostate": (a) tramples the Son of God under foot—rejects Christ; (b) such a person takes lightly the solemn shedding of covenant blood—regards the blood as a common thing; and (c) insults the Spirit of grace (the Holy Spirit), who brings the grace of God to humanity.
19. "Having therefore, brethren, boldness to enter into the holiest by the blood of Jesus, By a new and living way, which he hath consecrated for us, through the veil, that is to say, his flesh; And having an high priest over the house of God; Let us draw near with a true heart in full assurance of faith, having our hearts sprinkled from an evil conscience, and our bodies washed with pure water. Let us hold fast the profession of our faith without wavering; (for he is faithful that promised;) And let us consider one another to provoke unto love and to good works" (Hebrews 10:19–24, KJV).
20. Answers will vary.

ANSWER KEY TO LESSON 2

1. g
2. f
3. j
4. h
5. a
6. d
7. b
8. i
9. e
10. c
11. The stories of African Americans were left out of the news coverage of the terrorist attacks on September 11, 2001.
12. faith, believe, rely
13. Seven writers of the book of Psalms were: (a) David, (b) Asaph, (c) sons of Korah, (d) Moses, (e) Solomon, (f) Ethan, and (g) Herman.
14. f
15. (a) doubt, (b) persecution, (c) false teaching
16. Faith reveals the reality of God.
17. refuge
18. impossible
19. "Now faith is the substance of things hoped for, the evidence of things not seen" (Hebrews 11:1). "God is our refuge and strength, a very present help in trouble. Therefore will not we fear, though the earth be removed, and though the mountains be carried into

the midst of the sea; Though the waters thereof roar and be troubled, though the mountains shake with the swelling thereof. Selah" (Psalms 46:1–3).

20. Answers will vary.

ANSWER KEY TO LESSON 3

1. Alexandria: a city located in northern Africa where Apollos was born
2. chastening: education or training; by implication, it also means disciplinary correction
3. faith: endurance; the substance of things hoped
4. "Jesus is the 'finisher' of our faith": Jesus is the 'perfecter' of our faith.
5. patience: to remain under some trial so that we may be molded to fit God's purposes
6. perseverance: to be steadfast in a particular purpose
7. Rome: the capital city of Italy, it was the center of commerce, culture, and religion
8. sin: falling short of the mark; offense; falling short of God's standards
9. profit: to help to be profitable (gainful) or to be expedient
10. witness: one who can verify a particular truth based on what one has seen, heard, or knows
11. She cried out to God for help.
12. He wrote to: (a) inform his vacillating readers that Jesus Christ, the object of God's final revelation, is superior to the greatest of Judaism's heroes; and (b) to highlight and remind his audience of the efficacy of Jesus' power of salvation.
13. suffering, patience
14. Jesus Christ
15. Believers must develop endurance.
16. We should view trials suffered for righteousness' sake as the "chastening of the Lord" (Hebrews 12:5).
17. God's long-range goal in discipline is that we might be "partakers" of His holiness.
18. The purpose of the believer's pain is to produce Christlike behavior.
19. compassed, great, witnesses, lay aside, weight, sin, run, patience, race, Jesus, author, finisher, joy, cross, shame, right hand, God
20. Answers will vary.

ANSWER KEY TO LESSON 4

1. eschatology: end times, end things
2. ekklesia: the Greek word for "church"
3. "God's wrath": God as a "consuming fire."
4. innumerable: countless
5. mediator: one who intervenes between two; to restore peace and friendship
6. Mosaic Covenant: the conditions and requirements given by God to Moses on Mount Sinai for the Israelites to follow
7. Mount Sinai: where God gave the Law to the Israelites
8. Mount Zion: is reference to the "heavenly city" of God and believers who will dwell with Him
9. New Covenant: It is based upon Jesus Christ, the Mediator, who died for the sins of all humanity.
10. Septuagint: the first five books of the Old Testament (Genesis, Exodus, Leviticus, Numbers, and Deuteronomy)
11. Phillip told Samuel that he (Samuel) was blessed with life for a purpose—God had spared his life for a purpose.
12. gracious, merciful
13. Jews
14. faith, Lambs, Life
15. Jesus Christ
16. Jesus' blood opens up a way into the holiest for people—a way for humanity to be saved.
17. unbelief
18. gratitude, acceptable worship
19. "See that ye refuse not him that speaketh. For if they escaped not who refused him that spake on earth, much more shall not we escape, if we turn away from him that speaketh from heaven" (Hebrews 12:25).
20. Answers will vary.

ANSWER KEY TO LESSON 5

1. j
2. e
3. g
4. h
5. f
6. b
7. a

8. d
9. c
10. i
11. He was concerned that she did not love the members she served.
12. love
13. forgiveness
14. False
15. True
16. "Love is not easily provoked" means that love is neither touchy nor irritable; it thinks no evil, and does not store up the memory or keep an account of any wrong it has received. It puts away hurts of the past.
17. patience, kindness, and honesty
18. maturity, love
19. (a) "And though I bestow all my goods to feed the poor, and though I give my body to be burned, and have not charity, it profiteth me nothing" (1 Corinthians 13:3); (b) Answers will vary.
20. Answers will vary.

ANSWER KEY TO LESSON 6

1. e
2. j
3. g
4. f
5. d
6. b
7. a
8. i
9. c
10. h
11. power, grace
12. Paul, Barnabas
13. The problem arose over the distribution of gifts to the widows; the Greek-speaking believers felt overlooked.
14. The apostles used the godly solution of appointing Greek-speaking Jewish Christians to take charge of distributing food and money to the widows and other poor among them.
15. (a) They accused Stephen of speaking against the temple in Jerusalem, and (b) they accused both Stephen and Jesus of trying to destroy the Old Testament law.
16. They were unable to contest Stephen's amazing presentation of the Gospel of Jesus Christ.
17. Stephen showed through his words and ministry that the Law was fulfilled in Jesus; there was no more need to sacrifice the lives of animals to pay for their sins.
18. death, resurrection
19. full, faith, power, wonders, miracles
20. Answers will vary.

ANSWER KEY TO LESSON 7

1. Abram (Abraham): He was old and childless, but still believed that God would give him descendants, and God did (Isaac—the Israelites—God's chosen people)!
2. blasphemy: to slander or speak lightly of the divine
3. "miraculous signs: miracles that point to the grace and power of God
4. Moses: God used him to deliver His [God's] chosen people out of Egypt
5. Saul: later known as Paul; he persecuted Christians before being saved; they laid Stephen's clothes at his feet
6. "Son of Man": a title for Christ quoted from the book of Daniel
7. Stephen: the first Christian martyr; he died at the hands of the same people who had delivered Jesus to be crucified
8. "stiff-necked": stubborn, hardheaded
9. "uncircumcised heart": an unrepentant heart; a heart insensitive to the grace and glory of God
10. witnesses: those who confirm or give confirmation
11. True
12. history, Israel
13. Three accusations Stephen made against his detractors were: (a) they were stiff-necked as their ancestors had been; (b) their hearts were not circumcised—they lacked a spiritual relationship with God; and (c) they were resistant to God's Spirit.
14. Isaiah was cut in half.
15. They stoned Jeremiah.
16. False
17. God
18. At the time of Stephen's death, Paul was consenting and beginning his vigorous persecution of Christians.

19. "But he, being full of the Holy Ghost, looked up stedfastly into heaven, and saw the glory of God, and Jesus standing on the right hand of God, And said, Behold, I see the heavens opened, and the Son of man standing on the right hand of God" (Acts 7:55–56).
20. Answers will vary.

ANSWER KEY TO LESSON 8

1. Answers will vary.
2. Answers will vary.
3. Answers will vary.
4. Answers will vary.
5. Answers will vary.
6. Answers will vary.
7. Mr. Jones thought that because he was a big giver, he would automatically be elected.
8. Answers will vary.
9. history, faith Christianity
10. Philip's, Christ
11. (a) the kingdom of God and (b) Jesus Christ
12. The apostles send Peter and John to: (a) investigate and (b) to welcome the people of Samaria into the church.
13. Holy Spirit
14. "Simony" means, "trying to buy spiritual gifts or purchase an ecclesiastical office."
15. "But Peter said unto him, Thy money perish with thee, because thou hast thought that the gift of God may be purchased with money. Thou hast neither part nor lot in this matter: for thy heart is not right in the sight of God" (Acts 8:20–21).
16. Answers will vary.

ANSWER KEY TO LESSON 9

1. d
2. f
3. j
4. e
5. h
6. a
7. b
8. c
9. g
10. i
11. Ethiopian eunuch
12. bold, relentless
13. Jerusalem, Judea, Samaria, uttermost, parts, earth
14. Holy Spirit, Christ, Samaritans
15. obedience
16. Prayer, study, God's Word
17. God
18. (a) humiliation, exaltation; (b) Jesus' humiliation was His suffering and dying on the Cross; His exaltation was His resurrection.
19. believest, all thine heart, I believe, Jesus Christ, Son, God
20. Answers will vary.

ANSWER KEY TO LESSON 10

1. j
2. f
3. g
4. b
5. h
6. i
7. d
8. c
9. a
10. e
11. never
12. persecution, fortify, stand, Jesus'
13. Jewish
14. Jews, heretic
15. Paul was falsely accused of: (a) inciting Christians to riot against Jews; (b) being the ringleader of a sect of zealots intent on overthrowing the Romans; (c) insulting the Temple; and (d) insulting the priests and custodians.
16. According to Paul, the Bible's three most important definitions of true repentance and conversion are: (a) it begins with remorse for one's sin and turning away from the sin; (b) the sinner turns to God; and (c) the confirmation of honest repentance that gives one's testimony credibility is "works meets for repentance" (walk in God's Word).
17. Paul felt that (a) he experienced divine deliverance

many times as he encountered hardships and persecution, even while beaten and arrested, and (b) he had confidence in God's leadership and explained his skill in spreading Christ's message came from God.

18. life, death, resurrection
19. help, God, continue, witnessing, small, great, prophets, Moses, Christ, suffer, first, rise, dead, shew light, Gentiles
20. Answers will vary.

ANSWER KEY TO LESSON 11

1. Adramyttium: a port city at the northeast corner of the Aegean Sea
2. Aritarchus: one of Paul's Christian converts, who boarded the ship with Paul
3. Caesarea: where Paul spent two years under house arrest
4. delivered: handing a prisoner into someone's custody
5. fasting: a lack of appetite or available food
6. health: denotes salvation or deliverance
7. Julius: a centurion guarding the prisoners
8. Luke: the writer of the book of Acts and Luke's Gospel
9. meat: nourishment
10. willing: action one wants and is determined to take
11. Drew's faith in Jesus Christ enabled him to respond to his life storm with cheerfulness, not bitterness.
12. confidence, faithfulness
13. Caesar
14. An angel told Paul that they would be shipwrecked, but no one on board would die.
15. (a) call on God during crisis; (b) anticipate God's salvation; (c) listen to God's instruction; and (d) make known God's promises
16. d
17. They planned to kill them all.
18. credibility, authenticity, faith
19. bread, gave, thanks, God, presence, all, they all, good cheer
20. Answers will vary.

ANSWER KEY TO LESSON 12

1. barbarous: non-Greek speaking foreigners
2. Dike: the Greek goddess of justice
3. flux: a bowel sickness, such as dysentery
4. "Good Samaritans": people who come along side and help those in need
5. "making God's love real in action": showing God's love by helping others (letting others see the Jesus in you)
6. "minister": to reach out and help others
7. Malta: also called Melita; it is an island located near both Sicily and Syracuse and was in a strategic location for trade
8. "philanthropia": means "brotherly love"
9. Publius: Malta's leading citizen or government official
10. Zeus: the supreme Greek god
11. God, Good Samaritans
12. The islanders believed it was divine payback for some perceived crime.
13. True
14. False
15. The Maltese citizens expected Paul to die.
16. False
17. Two important lessons are: (a) while all people are sinners, that doesn't mean that they are bad people, and (b) it is important for each Christian to consistently make God's love visible in order to give our verbal witness an attractive credibility.
18. True
19. Publius, sick, fever, bloody flux, Paul, prayed, laid, hands, healed, others, diseases, came, healed
20. Answers will vary.

ANSWER KEY TO LESSON 13

1. j
2. d
3. g
4. f
5. h
6. i
7. a
8. b
9. e
10. c
11. imprisoned, commitment, Gospel, Christ

12. He wanted to acknowledge the common Jewish blood he shared with them.
13. Paul explained that he was bound because of the hope of Israel, which is the Messiah (Jesus Christ).
14. kingdom, God
15. True
16. c
17. God's salvation plan came to the Jews first, but when many of them did not choose to accept Jesus Christ as their Messiah—as their Lord and Savior—His salvation then went to the Gentiles, who accepted their salvation.
18. Their unbelief caused them to be rejected.
19. "Be it known therefore unto you, that the salvation of God is sent unto the Gentiles, and that they will hear it" (Acts 28:28).
20. Answers will vary.

DECEMBER 2022-FEBRUARY 2023

ANSWER KEY TO LESSON 1

1. chosen: to pick out; to select
2. dispensation: refers to God's plan of salvation, which He is bringing to pass in the "fullness of time"
3. forgiveness: the cancellation of an obligation—namely the obligation of payment for our sin
4. glory: brightness; splendor; majesty; to fame, renown, and honor
5. "God's incredible grace": God's favor
6. holy: consecrated; set apart; morally perfect; without blame
7. praise: the words of recognition that are due God for His work to save His people
8. predestinated: to decide upon beforehand; to predetermine; to foreordain
9. redemption: to set free from imprisonment or slavery for a ransom
10. "sealed": to mark for the purpose of identification or indicating ownership—a guarantee of authenticity
11. Joy was 4-years-old and had a tiny birthmark on the side of her cheek
12. redemption, Son, Jesus Christ
13. Rome
14. The vast plan of redemption is revealed from eternity before creation to the time of its future completeness at the time of Christ's Second Advent.
15. purposed, planned, accomplished, obligation, compulsion, merciful, compassionate
16. Paul praises God for His plan of redemption. He blesses God because God has blessed us through Christ Jesus.
17. A "biblical mystery" is a secret that God has not previously disclosed.
18. hearing, word, truth
19. "According as he hath chosen us in him before the foundation of the world, that we should be holy and without blame before him in love: Having predestinated us unto the adoption of children by Jesus Christ to himself, according to the good pleasure of his will (Ephesians 1:4–5).
20. Answers will vary.

ANSWER KEY TO LESSON 2

1. d
2. j
3. h
4. g
5. a
6. c
7. i
8. f
9. e
10. b
11. Jews, Gentiles, Ephesian
12. Gentiles had to remain in the outer court.
13. When Jesus was crucified, the curtain of the "Holy of Holies" was torn.
14. oneness, church
15. True
16. Apostle Paul was speaking of Christ, and one of His titles is "Prince of Peace."
17. gender, social, racial
18. According to the apostle Paul, three things that Christ has done through His blood to bring about unification in the Body of Christ are: (a) He has reconciled both Jews and Gentiles unto God in one body by the Cross;

(b) He created a new humanity where everyone is equal to each other and thereby making peace (figuratively, slaying the enmity) between them; and (c) by this act of sacrifice, Christ reconciled this new society to God, their Creator.

19. "For he is our peace, who hath made both one, and hath broken down the middle wall of partition between us; Having abolished in his flesh the enmity, even the law of commandments contained in ordinances; for to make in himself of twain one new man, so making peace; And that he might reconcile both unto God in one body by the cross, having slain the enmity thereby: And came and preached peace to you which were afar off, and to them that were nigh" (Ephesians 2:14-17).

20. Answers will vary.

ANSWER KEY TO LESSON 3

1. apostle: refers to the ones who were eyewitnesses to the risen Lord, chosen and authorized by Christ
2. edify: to build up the body of Christ
3. evangelist: preachers or those who proclaim the Gospel
4. forbearing: putting up with; to endure and bear with someone's mistakes or attitude
5. "lowliness of mind": a state of mind that recognizes the value of others
6. meekness: gentleness
7. prophets: they have special ability from God to give guidance to the Christian community and to declare the will of God
8. "spiritual gifts": the skills and abilities given to all believers by the Father through His Spirit
9. vocation: invitation calling
10. "walk worthy": everyday conduct that makes the connection between God's plan for us and our acceptance of that plan, as demonstrated in the way we live
11. Answers will vary.
12. Answers will vary.
13. True
14. False
15. love
16. A healthy formula for keeping the unity in the body of Christ is threefold: (a) unity in those things, which are essential to the faith; (b) liberty in those matters, which are nonessential or not absolute; and (c) charity (love) in all circumstances.
17. The unity of the Church arises from the unity of the Godhead because (a) the Church is one body because there is one Spirit who created it—the unity of this body is due to the work of the Holy Spirit who also indwells it; (b) the reality of the Christian calling and hope is founded on the one Lord, Jesus Christ who is the object of our faith (one faith), and in whom we all are baptized; and (c) the Church is described as one family in which every believer belongs because there is only one God who is the Father of all, who is above all, and through all, and in you all.
18. truth, love
19. unity, Spirit, bond, peace, one body, one Spirit, one hope, One Lord, one faith, one baptism, One God, Father, all, all, all, all every one, grace, gift, Christ
20. Answers will vary.

ANSWER KEY TO LESSON 4

1. angels: created beings whose primary purpose is to serve and worship God
2. Elizabeth: Mary's cousin, the wife of Zechariah, and the mother of John the Baptist
3. Gabriel: the angel who told Zechariah that he and Elizabeth were going to have a special child and they were going to have a special child and they were to name him "John"
4. "handmaiden": means "female slave"
5. immutable: unchangeable (the unchangeable God)
6. John the Baptist: Zechariah and Elizabeth's son; a forerunner of Jesus Christ – prepare the way
7. "Magnificat": Mary's hymn of praise
8. "magnify": glorify
9. soul: the seat of feelings, emotion, desire, and affection
10. strophes: stanzas of a hymn
11. loving, faithful
12. cherubim, seraphim
13. b
14. (a) Verses 46-49 speak of God's grace or favor on Mary; (b) verses 50-53 talk about what God has done in the life of the people of Israel; and (c) verses 54–55 are about God's faithfulness in keeping His promise to Abraham by sending the Messiah.
15. favor, honor
16. (a) immutability (unchangeable), (b) omnipotence (all-powerfulness), and (c) holiness (set apart from sin)

17. His mercy
18. (a) omnipotence (all-powerfulness), (b) holiness, (c) mercy, (d) justice, and (e) faithfulness
19. "And Mary said, My soul doth magnify the Lord, And my spirit hath rejoiced in God my Saviour. For he hath regarded the low estate of his handmaiden: for, behold, from henceforth all generations shall call me blessed" (Luke 1:46–48).
20. Answers will vary.

ANSWER KEY TO LESSON 5

1. e
2. f
3. h
4. b
5. i
6. d
7. j
8. a
9. c
10. g
11. Angie bowed her head over the papers and wept.
12. love, Christ, transform
13. grace, humility, submission
14. heart, attitude, obligation
15. head of the household
16. self sacrificing
17. nurture, protect, emotionally, physically, psychologically, spiritually
18. love, reverence
19. (a) "Wives, submit yourselves unto your own husbands, as unto the Lord; Husbands, love your wives, even as Christ also loved the church, and gave himself for it"; (b) Explanations will vary, but should include the wife cooperating and respecting her husband, and the husband loving his wife unconditionally as he loves himself as Christ loves the Church.
20. Answers will vary.

ANSWER KEY TO LESSON 6

1. g
2. c
3. f
4. i
5. h
6. b
7. d
8. j
9. e
10. a
11. It was important to Warren that he would be able to praise the Lord throughout this ordeal.
12. As we meet the challenges of life, people are watching to see if we are for real.
13. People could be imprisoned for: (a) nonpayment of debt; (b) political insurrection; (c) criminal acts; and (d) for certain religious practices.
14. love, encouragement, instruction
15. True
16. False
17. Apostle Paul's two convictions were: (a) whatever happened to him, he would not be ashamed, and (b) that he would wax bold in proclaiming the Gospel, as he had always done, but more so now that he was in prison—that Christ would be magnified.
18. faithful, lifted
19. earnest expectation, hope, ashamed, all boldness, Christ, magnified, my body, life, death, live, Christ, die, gain
20. Answers will vary.

ANSWER KEY TO LESSON 7

1. "agape love": to do good for another regardless of the cost to self
2. "Christ came into existence 'in the likeness of man'": speaks of Jesus' incarnation as a human
3. exalted: raising God to the highest point of honor
4. Jesus "being found in fashion as a man": Jesus is perceived or recognized as assuming the form and the role of a servant and the likeness and nature of a human being.
5. Jesus "made himself of no reputation": He voluntarily emptied out certain divine qualities and temporarily took on the human nature.
6. Jesus "taking the form of a servant": He exactly played the part of a servant of God.

7. Philippi: where Paul was miraculously delivered from bondage and the jailer was converted
8. Romans: They developed death by crucifixion.
9. servant: slave or bondsman
10. YAHWEH: the personal name of God
11. He learned that all that fuss was about what's good for her, not what's good for the church.
12. mind, Christ
13. internal strife, witness, Christ
14. unity, self-denial, Christ
15. Jesus emptied Himself of: (a) His equality with God; (b) His God-form—the Spiritual body, which He possessed in eternity and took on the human form; (c) His immortality; (d) the glory He had with the Father before the foundation of the world; (e) His authority in heaven and earth for all He did on earth He attributed it to the Father, and this was given back to Him after the resurrection; and (f) His divine attributes and power.
16. Put selfishness behind in doing God's work—be humble; in due times, He will exalt you.
17. Christ's super-exaltation means that He received the place of honor and majesty and is accordingly "seated at the right hand of God's throne" (Mark 16:19; Acts 2:33, 5:31; Romans 8:34; Hebrews 1:3).
18. (a) angels, (b) humans, (c) spirits, (d) demons, (e) principalities, and (f) powers
19. "Wherefore God also hath highly exalted him, and given him a name which is above every name: That at the name of Jesus every knee should bow, of things in heaven, and things in earth, and things under the earth; And that every tongue should confess that Jesus Christ is Lord, to the glory of God the Father" (Philippians 2:9–11)
20. Answers will vary.

ANSWER KEY TO LESSON 8

1. Paul was concerned about persons who trusted more in themselves and their accomplishments than in the person and works of Jesus Christ.
2. When Paul realized that "no legalistic training or adherence could save anyone," he gave up things, which was considered evil or worthless; He willingly walked away from a treasured lifestyle, held in high esteem by his family and community.
3. "To know Christ is not mere intellectual understanding of who He is." It is the most intimate relationship with Him; to know Christ is to experience His life.
4. The Pharisees were the most privileged and highly "respected" and "honored" people in the temple worship. They were ardent keepers of the law, and "blameless" in all aspects of the religion. However, they would not accept Jesus Christ as the Messiah.
5. Paul's quest to know Christ cost him everything, including the highest position, which he had attained within Judaism—being a Pharisee. He gave all this up.
6. Self-righteousness was Pharisaic righteousness, which is based on what one could do, not on what Christ did on the Cross.
7. Having Jesus Christ as his Lord and Savior really changed Grady's life.
8. The Libertines held a dual view of life—spiritual matter is good and physical matter is evil or worthless.
9. (a) Apostle Paul was circumcised on the eighth day, which meant he was born a Jew, not a proselyte; (b) he was "of the stock of Israel," meaning he was pure Hebrew, not of mixed descent as were many in Palestine during that day; (c) Paul was from the tribe of Benjamin, which had remained loyal to the Davidic line when the kingdom divided; and (d) he was a "Hebrew of the Hebrews," a phrase commonly used to designate those who had retained the national language.
10. (a) privilege, (b) family, (c) religious heritage, (d) his achievement, (e) rise to fame as a Pharisee, (f) power, (g) position
11. legalism, self-righteousness
12. The resurrection of Jesus Christ is important to us because: (a) His resurrection guarantees that our human bodies have great importance. It was in His earthly body that He died upon the Cross, and in His heavenly body that He rose again; (b) His resurrection is the guarantee that we shall rise again; (c) His resurrection blesses us with the wonderful joy of His promise to be with us forever.
13. death, imparted, believers
14. reflecting, life, likeness, Christ Jesus
15. "But what things were gain to me, those I counted loss for Christ. Yea doubtless, and I count all things but loss for the excellency of the knowledge of Christ Jesus my Lord: for whom I have suffered the loss of all things, and do count them but dung, that I may win Christ" (Philippians 3:7–8).
16. Answers will vary.

ANSWER KEY TO LESSON 9

1. g
2. c
3. f
4. i
5. h
6. d
7. e
8. j
9. b
10. a
11. Personal relationship with God
12. please, Lord, race
13. In Christ, there will be many winners.
14. The Lord told Ananias that apostle Paul would bring the name of Jesus before Gentiles, kings, and Jews.
15. The race was unfinished; there was a danger in looking back.
16. beginning, goal, process, lifetime
17. (a) He forgets the past; (b) He reaches forth—to stretch himself; and (c) He presses on toward the mark—the finish line.
18. (a) In the earthly race, the prize is perishable; in the heavenly race, the prize is imperishable (1 Corinthians 9:25); (b) In the earthly race, only one person wins the first prize (1 Corinthians 9:24); in the heavenly race, everyone who loves the appearing of Christ is a winner (2 Timothy 4:8); and (c) On earth, the fastest wins, while in heaven, whoever remains on the course, in spite of the time one starts or ends or at what pace one runs, wins.
19. apprehended, forgetting, behind, reaching, before, press toward, mark, prize, high calling, God
20. Answers will vary.

ANSWER KEY TO LESSON 10

1. j
2. e
3. d
4. g
5. a
6. i
7. c
8. f
9. h
10. b
11. Brenda viewed her life as a mess.
12. The lesson gives (a) a bigger picture of who Jesus is and (b) His position in the world.
13. Turkey
14. Epaphras
15. Christ
16. blood, forgiveness, sins
17. The phrase "He upholds and sustains all things" means, Christ sets everything into place, puts together everything, or unites the parts of everything into one whole.
18. The phrase, "Christ is the firstborn from the dead," means that He is the first person among the dead who would rise to life (His resurrection).
19. (a) him, all, created, heaven, earth, visible, invisible, thrones, dominions, principalities, powers, all, created, him, him; (b) Answers will vary, but should include that everything visible and invisible were made by a Sovereign God; He created them for Himself.
20. Answers will vary.

ANSWER KEY TO LESSON 11

1. circumcision: the cutting off of the foreskin
2. "established": to make firm; to make sure
3. "fullness": that which is put in to fill up; abundance
4. Gnosticism: a philosophy that did not want to attribute humanity to Jesus Christ
5. Godhead: Supreme deity; the essential being of God; the whole nature and attributes of God
6. receive: the doctrine passed down from the apostles to the faithful
7. rooted: rendered firm; fixed; established; firmly grounde
8. "stand firm": stick to foundational truths about Jesus Christ
9. vain: fruitless; of no purpose
10. "walk": the believer's daily life and habits
11. Tamika mistakenly felt that all religions lead to God.

12. fullness, Christ, rooted
13. flesh
14. Gnosticism (heretical teaching) was influencing believers and causing confusion.
15. planted, rooted, established
16. complete
17. heart, flesh
18. Because of Christ's death on the Cross for believers, God in His amazing mercy wipes away the record of our sins, and it is just as though we had never sinned.
19. dead, sins, uncircumcision, flesh, forgiven, all, trespasses, Blotting out, ordinances, nailing, his cross
20. Answers will vary.

ANSWER KEY TO LESSON 12

1. blasphemy: evil speaking against God or slander against humans
2. covetousness: a greedy desire to have more or to have what belongs to another
3. fornication: includes all manner of illicit sexual relationships or sexual intercourse
4. impurity: uncleanness in thought, word, and act
5. longsuffering: slowness in avenging wrongs
6. malice: a vicious disposition; a spirit that desires to injure one's neighbor
7. "mortify": put to death; to slay or kill
8. perfectness: completeness and bond
9. sanctification: to seek and set our affection on things above, not on things on the earth
10. Scythians: rude or rough; the lowest class of barbarian
11. take off, old life, new one
12. dead
13. evil passions, desires, practices
14. To "put on the new man" is to wear as garments the new nature, which results from our spiritual union with Christ through His death and resurrection (2 Corinthians 5:17).
15. "Chosen or elect" of God means that believers are "set apart ones, special or sacred or saints"—holy.
16. "Longsuffering" is "slowness in avenging wrongs—it characterizes a person who refuses to yield to passion and rage in the face of wrongs done to him or her—a person who has self-control."
17. peace, hearts
18. teach, admonish, psalms, hymns, spiritual songs
19. elect, holy, mercies, kindness, humbleness of mind, meekness, longsuffering; Forbearing, forgiving, charity
20. Answers will vary.

ANSWER KEY TO LESSON 13

1. e
2. d
3. f
4. i
5. b
6. c
7. j
8. g
9. a
10. h
11. Felicia almost never prayed and when things went wrong in her life, she did not feel the presence of God.
12. vital
13. He was in prison.
14. (a) He exhorts believers to make sure their lives reflect Christ; (b) to not focus on earthly things but on things of God because they have a new life in Christ; and (c) he encouraged them to put aside the various sins of their old selves.
15. prayer
16. True
17. False
18. faith
19. "Walk in wisdom toward them that are without, redeeming the time. Let your speech be always with grace, seasoned with salt, that ye may know how ye ought to answer every man" (Colossians 4:5-6).
20. Answers will vary.

MARCH-MAY 2023

ANSWER KEY TO LESSON 1

1. beheld: saw, or in a vision or dream, it means to witness.
2. Cyrus: king of Persia
3. Darius: the king who was tricked into throwing Daniel into the lions' den
4. eschatology: end-time prophesies
5. horn: metaphorically signifies strength and honor; symbolic use in visions for kings and kingdoms
6. Nebuchadnezzar: king of Babylon
7. sovereignty: royalty, reign, kingship, or kingdom
8. the "Ancient of Days": lifetime or eternity; characterizes God as a judge whose reign is eternal
9. "the Daniel fast": Daniel only ate fruits and vegetables.
10. the "Son of man": the Messiah—Jesus Christ
11. Regina told Marcus and Felicia that becoming financially intimate with her own husband was the best thing that she could ever have done.
12. In today's lesson, Daniel's dream foreshadowed better days ahead.
13. It was also given to apostle John (Revelation 20:11–15).
14. Daniel advocated that believers should keep being faithful to God.
15. hope
16. eternal
17. fire
18. It represented the last of earth's evil rulers, called "the beast."
19. "And there was given him dominion, and glory, and a kingdom, that all people, nations, and languages, should serve him: his dominion is an everlasting dominion, which shall not pass away, and his kingdom that which shall not be destroyed" (Daniel 7:14).
20. Answers will vary.

ANSWER KEY TO LESSON 2

1. g
2. f
3. e
4. b
5. i
6. h
7. j
8. a
9. d
10. c
11. She was arrested for filing fraudulent claims.
12. Daniel went to God in prayer on behalf of his people.
13. Jeremiah
14. Daniel was concerned about the hearts of the people.
15. Daniel had prepared himself for such a solemn prayer by: (a) fasting, (b) mourning, and (c) wearing sackcloth.
16. model prayer, penitence
17. faithful
18. sinners
19. "To the Lord our God belong mercies and forgiveness, though we have rebelled against him" (Daniel 9:9).
20. Answers will vary.

ANSWER KEY TO LESSON 3

1. "after many days": in the distant future
2. Antiochus Epiphanes: a contemptible ruler who ran roughshod over the Jews
3. epiphany: a pre-incarnate appearance of Christ
4. eschatology: end times
5. Gabriel: an angel sent by God to Daniel to explain Daniel's visions
6. indignation: anger, rage, or wrath
7. "the animals": refer to kings or kingdoms of the world in Daniel's visions
8. "the indignation": Epiphanes' destruction of Jerusalem, the butchering of 80,000 Jews, and his vile desecration of the Temple, where he not only erected a statue of Zeus Olympios but sacrificed pigs on the holy altar
9. "the ram": represented the Medo-Persian Empire in Daniel's vision
10. "the two horns": represented Kings Darius and Cyrus in Daniel's vision
11. Andre was ashamed to be 40 and have nothing to show for it.

12. "If you want things to be different, you gotta do different things."
13. (a) a ram, (b) a goat, and (c) a little horn
14. comfort
15. (a) God, (b) heaven, and (c) the church
16. "the Illustrious God, "the Madman"
17. self-centered, God-centered
18. overcome, prevail
19. I, make, be, last end, indignation, appointed
20. Answers will vary.

ANSWER KEY TO LESSON 4

1. determined: appointed, decreed, or ordained
2. Eucharist: Communion, the Lord's Supper; the offering of thanksgiving to God for what He has done in salvation
3. Jerusalem: both the religious and the political seat of Palestine, and the place where the Messiah was expected to arrive
4. Judas: the disciple who betrayed Jesus to His killers
5. Passion of Christ: Christ's suffering for believers on the Cross
6. "Passover Lamb": Jesus Christ
7. remembrance: a recollection
8. serve: to be an attendant
9. "The Feast of Unleavened Bread": commemorates the Israelites' haste to leave Egypt, which did not allow them to use yeast and then wait for their bread to rise
10. "the Passover": commemorates the death angel passing over the house of the Israelites while they were in Egypt because they had the blood of the lamb on their doorposts
11. Michelle believed it was important to give back to the community since God had blessed her with a good job; at first Regina did not believe this.
12. servants
13. They felt that the large crowds might rise up and stone them for hurting Jesus.
14. forgiven, death, sin
15. sinners
16. Suffering Servant
17. lower place
18. His coming kingdom
19. "And he took bread, and gave thanks, and brake it, and gave unto them, saying, This is my body which is given for you: this do in remembrance of me" (Luke 22:19).
20. Answers will vary.

ANSWER KEY TO LESSON 5

1. f
2. e
3. g
4. h
5. a
6. i
7. c
8. j
9. d
10. b
11. Regina needed to hear from the dead girl's mother that part of the girl would live on in her son, Emmanuel.
12. hope
13. True
14. suffer, die on the Cross, resurrected
15. They thought that Jesus would become their earthly king and overthrow the government.
16. persecution
17. False
18. lords, kings
19. (a) "And they rose up the same hour, and returned to Jerusalem, and found the eleven gathered together, and them that were with them, Saying, The Lord is risen indeed, and hath appeared to Simon" (Luke 24:33–34). (b) Answers will vary.
20. Answers will vary.

ANSWER KEY TO LESSON 6

1. f
2. h
3. g
4. e
5. b

6. j
7. d
8. a
9. c
10. i
11. Christian
12. promises, fulfilled all
13. (c) third
14. His nail-pierced hands and feet
15. faith, sight
16. suffering, death, resurrection
17. atonement, sins
18. Teacher, Master, Lord
19. Christ, suffer, rise, dead, third, repentance, remission, sins, all nations, Jerusalem, witnesses
20. Answers will vary.

ANSWER KEY TO LESSON 7

1. confounded: stirred up or thrown into disorder
2. devout: reverencing God; pious, religious
3. Holy Ghost: the Third Person of the Holy Trinity—Father, Son, and Holy Ghost; also called the Holy Spirit
4. mighty: violent, forcible
5. mocking: deriding, jeering
6. Pentecost: a commemoration of the descent of the Holy Spirit and the outpouring of the gifts of the Spirit
7. proselytes: Gentiles who had been converted to Judaism
8. "Shavuot": the Jewish holiday "the Feast of Weeks", which celebrates Moses receiving the Ten Commandments on Mount Sinai
9. "transforming power": the Holy Spirit provides life transforming power—power to be what God has called us to be.
10. wind: breath
11. Michelle launched a visitation and outreach program for the elderly in her community.
12. lost, hurting souls
13. e
14. Some believe that the Day of Pentecost marked the beginning of the Christian church.
15. (a) The apostles were all gathered together in one place, and (b) they were all of one accord.
16. The visible evidence of the presence of the Holy Spirit was what appeared to be flames that lit upon all of them.
17. (a) "Being filled with the Spirit" is a repeated experience and (b) "the Baptism of the Spirit" is a one-time experience.
18. Some accused those whom God had filled with the Spirit as being filled with new wine.
19. "And when the day of Pentecost was fully come, they were all with one accord in one place. And suddenly there came a sound from heaven as of a rushing mighty wind, and it filled all the house where they were sitting. And there appeared unto them cloven tongues like as of fire, and it sat upon each of them. And they were all filled with the Holy Ghost, and began to speak with other tongues, as the Spirit gave them utterance" (Acts 2:1–4).
20. Answers will vary.

ANSWER KEY TO LESSON 8

1. "The day of the Lord will come like a thief in the night" is a metaphor that illustrates that the Day of the Lord will begin when it is least expected.
2. "The time would occur when people are expecting 'peace and safety'" suggests that there will be calm before the storm.
3. "Apostle Paul described the unbelieving world as living in darkness," unknowing, unable to perceive when it comes to end time events.
4. "Apostle Paul described believers as 'children of the light'"—those who eagerly anticipate the return of Christ and live each day as though today will be the day.
5. Apostle Paul tells believers to put on their Christian armor and prepare for combat so that no matter what the world throws at us, be it trouble, persecution, hardship, or even the threat of death, we will be more than conquerors through Christ who loves us.
6. Christians have adopted the word "parousia" to mean the second coming of the Lord. He came the first time as Lord and Savior. He is returning the second time as Judge. He is returning in all His glory.
7. Thieves never show up when people are looking for them.
8. Believers are to live as though we expect Christ to return at any moment.

9. Timothy
10. He addressed the issue of whether those who had died before Jesus' second coming would have the possibility of sharing in the kingdom of God at the time of His return.
11. (a) breastplate—it is to guard our hearts so that we will not allow the world's situations to become issues that affect our hearts; (b) the helmet, the hope of salvation—believers should hope in their salvation—hope in Christ and His promise to never leave or forsake us. The salvation of Christ is guaranteed for eternity.
12. faith, love, hope
13. It expresses the result of God's "battle" on the believer's behalf.
14. wrath
15. "For the Lord himself shall descend from heaven with a shout, with the voice of the archangel, and with the trump of God: and the dead in Christ shall rise first: Then we which are alive and remain shall be caught up together with them in the clouds, to meet the Lord in the air: and so shall we ever be with the Lord" (1 Thessalonians 4:16–17).
16. Answers will vary.

ANSWER KEY TO LESSON 9

1. d
2. g
3. a
4. f
5. j
6. h
7. i
8. b
9. c
10. e
11. Warren realized that God does not call all of those that He equips through His Holy Spirit to work at churches that appear to have it all together—thriving spiritually and physically. God needs workers in churches that are struggling—that truly need the Physician, God.
12. God's agenda is saving lost souls, helping to build His kingdom.
13. (a) Apostle Paul wrote to encourage the Thessalonians, who were experiencing persecution and (b) to correct the false information about Jesus' second coming.
14. (a) the coming of the man of sin or lawlessness and (b) open rebellion against God
15. favor, gift
16. compassion, mercy, chose, heirs
17. (a) Study God's Word in context; (b) cross-reference Scriptures in order to know what the Bible actually says or teaches; (c) read the Scriptures surrounding the text (e.g., the entire chapter, the book the chapter is contained in; and (d) consider the people, places, and times of that Scripture—what was happening at the time.
18. established
19. bound, thanks alway, God, God, chosen, salvation, sanctification, truth
20. Answers will vary.

ANSWER KEY TO LESSON 10

1. f
2. e
3. j
4. g
5. a
6. h
7. i
8. d
9. c
10. b
11. Robert determined to: (a) trust God and (b) take one day at a time.
12. resurrection
13. True
14. Jesus Christ
15. power, God, faith
16. Suffering in a believer's life (a) tests his/her faith and (b) brings it to maturity.
17. False
18. repentance, forgiveness
19. (a) trial, faith, precious, gold, tried, fire, praise, honour, glory, Jesus Christ; (b) Answers will vary.
20. Answers will vary.

ANSWER KEY TO LESSON 11

1. brotherly kindness: love of people
2. charity: godly love
3. corruption: ruin by moral influences; depravity
4. faith: belief in God and His finished work at Calvary; what brings us to Christ in the first place
5. godliness: reverence or piety
6. knowledge: discernment or a firm grasp of truth
7. patience: steadfastness, endurance
8. temperance: self-control
9. "the truth": God's Word
10. virtue: holy courage, strength
11. False
12. True
13. threatened, arrested, beaten, killed
14. He was murdered by a mob.
15. He was put to death on the orders of Herod Agrippa I.
16. He wrote to: (a) warn Christians about the many false teachers who were vying to take them off the foundational truths of the faith and (b) to exhort them to grow in the wisdom and knowledge of Jesus Christ—to grow in their faith.
17. growing, shaping, refining
18. grace, mercy, goodness, faith
19. virtue, virtue knowledge, knowledge temperance, temperance patience, patience godliness, godliness brotherly kindness, brotherly kindness charity
20. Answers will vary.

ANSWER KEY TO LESSON 12

1. body: the sinful nature in us
2. debauchery: corruption, wickedness, depravity
3. "God's grace": God's unmerited favor
4. holiness: set apart from sin
5. lasciviousness: depravity, iniquity, wickedness
6. love: agape love (unconditional)
7. "Pente": means 50
8. sanctification: consecrated, made holy
9. sober: clearheaded, restrained, serious
10. "the kingdom of God": the reign of God
11. Michelle was overjoyed as she prepared to minister to the needs of others in a foreign nation.
12. (a) Jerusalem, (b) Judaea, (c) Samaria, and (d) the uttermost part of the earth
13. They were waiting for the power from on high (the Holy Ghost).
14. (a) having been with Jesus from the time of John's baptism, (b) to be a witness of Jesus' resurrection, and (c) having beheld Jesus' ascension into heaven
15. Followers of Christ must put on the mind of Christ.
16. (a) be sober, (b) watchful, and (c) prayerful
17. the blood of Jesus
18. (a) the speaking gifts and (b) that of service
19. Christ, suffered, flesh, arm, same mind, suffered, flesh, ceased, sin, flesh, lusts, will, God
20. Answers will vary.

ANSWER KEY TO LESSON 13

1. e
2. g
3. j
4. f
5. b
6. i
7. d
8. a
9. c
10. h
11. A promise is a binding declaration between two or more people or institutions.
12. God
13. (a) He wrote to warn Christians about false teachers and (b) to exhort them to grow in their faith and in the knowledge of the Lord and Savior, Jesus Christ.
14. "The last days" refer to the period between the first and second coming of Christ.
15. God's Word
16. longsuffering
17. (a) the heavens will pass away with a great noise, (b) there will be elements melting, and (c) the earth (along with the works thereon) will burn up
18. (a) The new heaven and new earth (promised in

Isaiah 65:17) will be perfect because all traces and effects of sin will be completely wiped out, (b) Satan and his demons will be thrown into hell, and (c) no unrighteous person will gain admittance to the new heaven and new earth (1 Corinthians 6:9–10; Revelation 21:8).

19. "But, beloved, be not ignorant of this one thing, that one day is with the Lord as a thousand years, and a thousand years as one day. The Lord is not slack concerning his promise, as some men count slackness; but is longsuffering to us-ward, not willing that any should perish, but that all should come to repentance" (2 Peter 3:8–9).
20. Answers will vary.

JUNE-AUGUST 2023

ANSWER KEY TO LESSON 1

1. death: eternal separation from the living God
2. glory: God's presence
3. holy: transcendent; set apart from sin
4. iniquity: depravity, perversity, and the guilt from sin
5. Isaiah: the son of Amoz and a prophet of the southern kingdom of Judah
6. King Uzziah: also known as Azariah, began his long reign in 783 B.C.
7. "train": the skirt or the hem of a robe
8. "the seraphim": majestic beings with six wings, human hands, or voices in attendance upon God
9. undone: on the verge of perishing in the face of a holy God
10. woe: a passionate cry of grief or despair
11. They worshiped God and voiced their complete trust in the Lord to see His company through this tough time as God had done so many times before.
12. Warren praised God for giving him the insight to solve the company's problem.
13. Amos, Hosea in Israel, Isaiah, and Micah in Judah
14. holiness
15. sinfulness
16. grace
17. call
18. holy authority, love
19. "Then said I, Woe is me! for I am undone; because I am a man of unclean lips, and I dwell in the midst of a people of unclean lips: for mine eyes have seen the King, the LORD of hosts" (Isaiah 6:5).
20. Answers will vary.

ANSWER KEY TO LESSON 2

1. e
2. f
3. i
4. h
5. g
6. b
7. d
8. a
9. j
10. c
11. When Grandma Jean shared old pictures and stories about their family's history.
12. gratitude, God, blessings.
13. (a) Isaiah, (b) Micah
14. They will praise Him for (a) the final restoration of Israel and (b) unification of His divided and scattered church.
15. He praised God for His great love, which caused Him to turn away his anger toward disobedient people and to instead bless them with divine favor.
16. (a) security, (b) confidence, (c) hope
17. He instructed them to call upon the Lord.
18. Isaiah instructed the inhabitants of Zion to cry out and should because "great is the Holy One of Israel in the midst of thee."
19. "Behold, God is my salvation; I will trust, and not be afraid: for the LORD JEHOVAH is my strength and my song; he also is become my salvation" (Isaiah 12:2).
20. Answers will vary.

ANSWER KEY TO LESSON 3

1. blindness: unable to see truth (both soul and spirit can be blind)
2. counsel: consultation, purpose, plans, designs, and wisdom
3. heart: the center of man's inner or immaterial nature; the whole spectrum of human emotion is attributed to the heart

4. mouth: a manifestation of an individual's character and disposition whether good or bad
5. omnipotent: God is all powerful
6. omnipresent: God is all present; present everywhere
7. omniscient: God is all knowing
8. "stay yourself": question oneself or to be hesitant to do what is right; to be reluctant to obey what has been commanded; to linger or delay in complying with God's Word
9. "stumbling block": leaders who cause God's people to forsake true worship and turn to false or insincere worship
10. vision: revelation or insight from God
11. life giver
12. Spirit, truth
13. ineffective
14. rebellion
15. disobedience
16. omniscient, omnipresent, omnipotent
17. reshape, reshaped
18. offense
19. draw near me, mouth, lips, honour, removed, heart, precept
20. Answers will vary.

ANSWER KEY TO LESSON 4

1. cosmologists: scientists who study the physical universe
2. create: to form, produce, engrave
3. earth: the planet we live on, including its inhabitants, land, and seas
4. glad: "sus'" in Hebrew, meaning to make merry and exceedingly rejoice
5. heavens: the spiritual realm where God and the angels dwell
6. "Jerusalem's Prophetic Destiny": worship center when the promised time of renewal comes
7. "Milky Way": galaxy in which we live
8. rejoice: means "gil" in Hebrew
9. theologians: Bible scholars who study the nature of God an how He acts and influences the physical universe
10. trouble: "behalah" in Hebrew, meaning "fear, fright, sudden destruction, or the sudden terror of God brought upon disobedient Israel"
11. finite
12. heaven, earth, eternity
13. millennial, end-time
14. (a) eternal, (b) safe, (c) peaceful and (d) abundant
15. blessing
16. suffered
17. (a) humanity fell from grace, (b) humanity fell from God's gracious presence
18. pain, death
19. "For, behold, I create new heavens and a new earth: and the former shall not be remembered, nor come into mind. But be ye glad and rejoice for ever in that which I create: for, behold, I create Jerusalem a rejoicing, and her people a joy."
20. Answers will vary.

ANSWER KEY TO LESSON 5

1. f
2. h
3. g
4. e
5. b
6. i
7. j
8. c
9. a
10. d
11. He felt in his heart that God was not pleased.
12. joyful worship
13. fear
14. Thanksgiving, 40, tents, wilderness
15. King Cyrus of Persia
16. spirit
17. burnt offering
18. false
19. "And afterward offered the continual burnt offering, both of the new moons, and of all the set feasts of the

LORD that were consecrated, and of every one that willingly offered a freewill offering unto the LORD."

20. Answers will vary.

ANSWER KEY TO LESSON 6

1. e
2. j
3. a
4. h
5. f
6. c
7. i
8. b
9. d
10. g
11. joy, praise
12. triumph, His name, victory
13. f. 70 years
14. a) consecrate themselves, b) submit freewill offerings, c) provide the resources and talent to rebuild the temple
15. Rebuilding the Temple was the first step in regaining their statehood as a nation again under God's protective covering.
16. 16. They wept because they had witnessed the splendor of the former Temple and how sin led them into captivity. At the same time, they recognized the goodness of God and longed for His presence.
17. 17. True
18. 18. True
19. sang together, praising, giving thanks, LORD, good, mercy, for ever, shouted, shout, praised, foundation, laid
20. Answers will vary.

ANSWER KEY TO LESSON 7

1. archetype: a pattern
2. "consecrate themselves": act by the children of Israel to remove all filthiness and unclean practices to seek the Lord their God
3. dedication: an inauguration, a dedicatory sacrifice
4. Feast of Unleavened Bread: closely associated with Passover
5. King Darius: reigned from about 522 to 485 B.C.
6. Passover: a sparing, an exemption, an immunity from penalty and calamity
7. prophesying: preaching, teaching and/or predicting the future
8. purified: de-sinned in order to be ceremonially clean
9. "sin offering": guilt offering presented for intentional and unintentional sins
10. "the perfect sacrifice": Jesus
11. They made sure to always have a prayer closet that they dedicated to the Lord for His many wonderful blessings.
12. Passover
13. King Cyrus
14. the royal treasury
15. because favor of the Lord helped them rebuild
16. God
17. a) 100 male bulls, b) 200 rams, c) 400 male lamb
18. It meant that they were all on one accord and as one unity ready to observe the proper rites and ceremonies.
19. "And the children of Israel, the priests, and the Levites, and the rest of the children of the captivity, kept the dedication of this house of God with joy" (Ezra 6:16).
20. Answers will vary.

ANSWER KEY TO LESSON 8

1. He led the people in prayer and fasting to ensure God's protection in the people's return to their homeland.
2. Ezra understood that many obstacles could arise and hinder the children of Israel on their journey.
3. Seeking God first can lead to clarity of what to do when a solution to a problem is unclear.
4. Sometimes the most obvious way isn't the way God would have us go.
5. Prayer is what makes a fast a fast and not a diet.
6. Ezra was a scribe, extremely familiar with the Word of God, had an intimate relationship with Him, assembled the people of Israel together and declared a national fast.
7. She found herself asking God for answers.
8. fasting, praying, dire

9. scribe, Mosaic Law
10. God's, exiles
11. 2,000; 720
12. God responded to their fasting and praying.
13. hearts, minds, humility, relying totally
14. hears, views, sincere heart, mind
15. "Then I proclaimed a fast there, at the river of Ahava, that we might afflict ourselves before our God, to seek of him a right way for us, and for our little ones, and for all our substance."
16. Answers will vary.

ANSWER KEY TO LESSON 9

1. g
2. f
3. i
4. j
5. h
6. b
7. a
8. d
9. e
10. c
11. He is thankful for how God kept him and how He continues to do so.
12. He financially supports the shelter and the soup kitchen, and he has paid for church repairs.
13. a) Egypt, b) Lebanon, c) Syria, d) Turkey, e) Jordan, f) Iraq, g) Iran
14. f. 58
15. holy to God
16. d. 80
17. holy
18. willing offering
19. Ye, holy, LORD, vessels, holy, silver, gold, freewill
20. Answers will vary.

ANSWER KEY TO LESSON 10

1. f
2. j
3. h
4. a
5. i
6. b
7. c
8. d
9. e
10. g
11. a) blowing a shofar to serve as an alarm, b) messengers going from household to household
12. Feast of Tabernacles
13. False
14. a) the books of the Law b) seven days
15. the eighth day
16. olive branches, myrtle, palm and other leafy trees
17. The people rejoiced at what had been done in their lives and, no doubt, at the realization of how connected they were through the religious rituals to the ancestors of old who had been brought out of Egypt.
18. The more they learned, the more they rejoiced over hearing the Word of God. The more they learned, the greater was their assurance that God was able to strengthen them because He had proven this time and again.
19. congregation, captivity, Jeshua, Nun, children of Israel, gladness
20. Answers will vary.

ANSWER KEY TO LESSON 11

1. f
2. d
3. e
4. g
5. a
6. j
7. b
8. c
9. i
10. h
11. a) confession of one's sin b) the reading and hearing of Scripture

12. repentance and belief in the death, burial, and resurrection of Jesus
13. True
14. Shechaniah, Jehiel, Ezra, trespassed, God, strange wives, hope, Israel
15. deliver, heal, empower, and transform
16. Nehemiah 9
17. God elected for Himself, not a group of worshiping individuals, but an entire covenant community.
18. Mount Ebal represents God's curse for disobedience.
19. "And the seed of Israel separated themselves from all strangers, and stood and confessed their sins, and the iniquities of their fathers" (Nehemiah 9:2).
20. Answers will vary.

ANSWER KEY TO LESSON 12

1. c
2. i
3. h
4. j
5. b
6. g
7. f
8. a
9. e
10. d
11. a) dignity, b) safety
12. God promised them after exile that they would return to their land and that He would restore them to fruitfulness, blessings, and plenty.
13. False
14. beseech, commandedst, Moses, scatter, commandments, cast out, heaven, gather, chosen
15. Because of their own disobedience, apostasy, and rebellion, God had removed them from their land and taken everything from them
16. with the music of cymbals, psalteries, and harps
17. Hoshaiah, half of the princes of Judah, Azariah, Ezra, Meshullam, Judah, Benjamin, Shemaiah, Jeremiah, Zechariah the son of Jonathan, the son of Shemaiah, the son of Mattaniah, the son of Michaiah, the son of Zaccur, the son of Asaph: and his brethren, Shemaiah, and Azarael, Milalai, Gilalai, Maai, Nethaneel, and Judah, Hanani, with the musical instruments of David the man of God, and Ezra the scribe before them
18. "Also that day they offered great sacrifices, and rejoiced: for God had made them rejoice with great joy: the wives also and the children rejoiced: so that the joy of Jerusalem was heard even afar off" (Nehemiah 12:43).
19. Answers will vary.

ANSWER KEY TO LESSON 13

1. g
2. d
3. j
4. i
5. h
6. a
7. c
8. e
9. b
10. f
11. a) trading, b) buying, c) selling
12. They were to show complete submission to Him as their King and total adoration of Him.
13. False
14. laws, ordinances, spiritual framework
15. Reading of the law sparked creation of a covenant that set out detailed obligations, which they would comply with in order to please God. This document set the legal framework for their establishment as a nation.
16. The keeping of the Sabbath was a sign that God truly ruled Israel.
17. To disobey the Sabbath meant to profane the holiness of the day, or to make it unclean or unholy.
18. He reminded them that such behavior originally contributed to their demise and exile from the Promised Land.
19. commanded, cleanse, sanctify, Remember me, spare me, greatness, mercy
20. Answers will vary.

NOTES

NOTES

NOTES

NOTES

NOTES

NOTES